Becoming
Independent

Becoming Independent

An East Tennessee Memoir

Ruth Johnson Smiley

© 2023 Ruth Johnson Smiley
Cover design by BespokeBookCovers.com
All rights reserved. The publisher requires prior written permission for any form of reproduction or transmission of this publication, including photocopying, recording, or use of any information storage or retrieval system.
Post Rock Press does not control or take responsibility for any third-party websites referred to or in this book. All internet addresses given in this book were correct at the time of going to press. The author and publisher regret any inconvenience caused if addresses have changed or sites have ceased to exist, but can accept no responsibility for any such changes.
This book is a memoir. It reflects the author's present recollections of experiences. In this memoir, the author altered some names and characteristics, condensed some events, and recreated some dialogue.

First Edition
ISBN: 979-8-9875793-3-6
Library of Congress Control Number: 2024906957

Post Rock Press
P.O. Box 24314
Knoxville, TN 37933

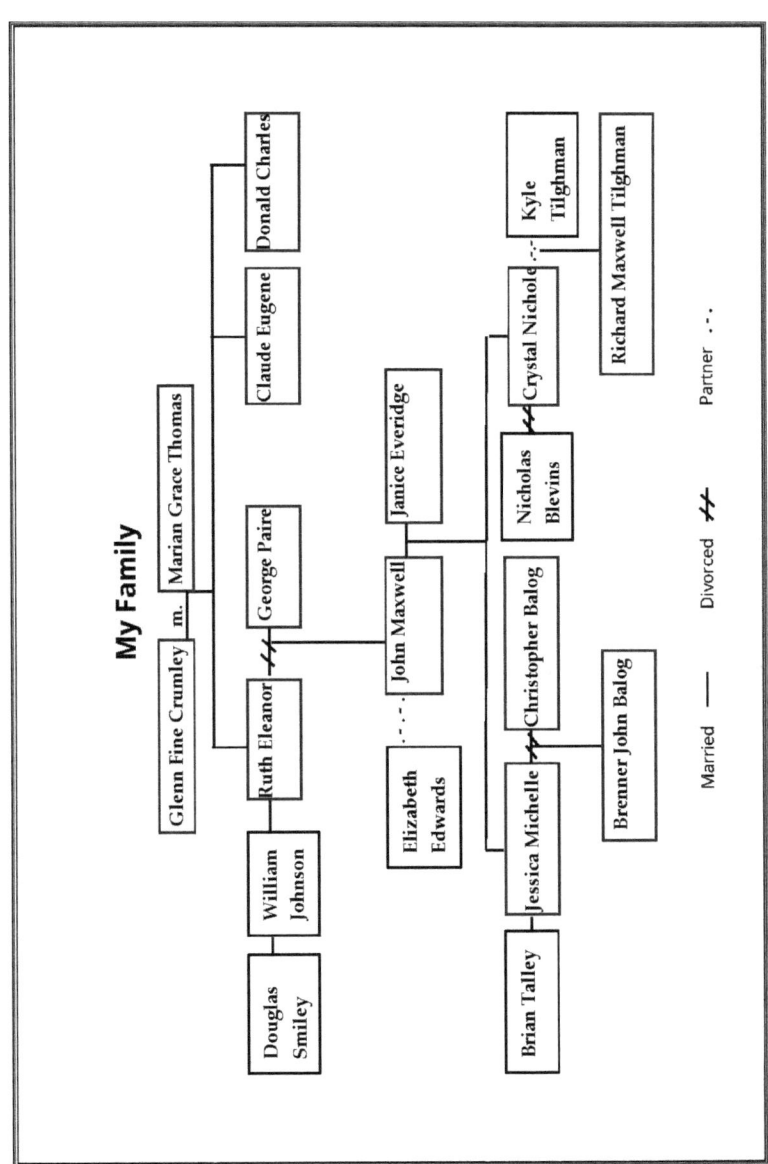

Figure 1. Family Chart, Ruth Johnson Smiley

Contents

CONTENTS	VII
GROWING UP	1
My Home in East Tennessee	3
Glenn Fine Crumley (1911-1994)	7
Marian Grace Thomas Crumley (1916-2006)	9
Glenn and Grace	10
Their First Child	12
A New House and a Second Child	15
A Third Child	17
Celebrating Holidays	19
More Memories	21
Reflections	31
MARRIAGE	35
Traditions and Expectations	37
George Edgar Paire (Married 1956-1968)	38

    Robert William Johnson (Married 1971-1995) 49

    Edwin Douglas Smiley (Married 1998-2022) 57

    Reflections 66

MY BABY BOY 67

    Becoming a Mother... 69

    Preparing for a Baby 69

    The Big Event... 71

    John's First Year 74

SCHOOL AND WORK..79

    Navigating Education and Jobs 81

    Weavers Elementary School (1942-1950)........................... 82

    Bluff City High School (1950-1954) 87

    The University of Tennessee (1954-1955) 96

    Inter-Mountain Telephone Company (1956) 101

    Tennessee Valley Bank (1956-1958).................................. 103

    The University of Tennessee (1958-1962) 105

    Oak Ridge Institute of Nuclear Studies (1963-1969)...... 107

    The University of Tennessee (1969-1971) 109

    Anderson County Day Care (1972-1973)......................... 112

    City of Oak Ridge (1973-1979) 112

The University of Tennessee and Oak Ridge National Laboratory (1979-1981) 114

Oak Ridge Associated Universities (1980-1982) 118

Economic System Analysis, Inc. (1983-1985) 120

Science & Technology, Inc. (1986-1988) 121

Pellissippi State Community College (1988-1993, 1996-1999) 123

Reflections 129

GRANDCHILDREN 131

Next Generations 133

The Greats and Grands 138

ORGANIZATIONS 141

Expanding Horizons 143

4-H Club (1946-1954) 143

American Association of University Women (AAUW) (1970-present) 146

Taoist Tai Chi (2014-present) 148

MY SPIRITUAL JOURNEY 151

The Power of Faith 153

EPILOGUE 157

ACKNOWLEDGEMENTS 159

PUBLICATIONS AND TECHNICAL REPORTS 161

MEDIA CREDITS 163
ABOUT THE AUTHOR 167

Growing Up

My Home in East Tennessee

East Tennessee has always been my home. I grew up on a farm near Bristol in Sullivan County. Then I went to Knoxville to attend the University of Tennessee, and I never left the Knoxville-Oak Ridge area. As a lifelong resident of Tennessee, I'm a minority in Oak Ridge where people come from every state and several foreign countries. And some grew up in East Tennessee, left, and then came back to the area they left behind. It's a good place to live with the beautiful mountains, lakes, and a few small historic towns. The area claims to be the birthplace of country music, as well as the birthplace of Davy Crockett and Dolly Parton. My German ancestors settled in what is now Sullivan County in the 1780s. They brought with them their German Bible, Lutheran faith, and love of the land.

I'm a proud member of First Families of Tennessee, a register of settlers who were here when Tennessee became a state in 1796 and direct descendants who document their lineage through birth certificates, census reports, deeds, and other official documents. I grew up with a large extended family including grandparents, aunts, uncles, and cousins, and I have fond memories of the times we spent together. I value the contacts I have today with my cousins, nieces, and nephews.

Figure 2. Ruth with parents Glenn and Grace Crumley at home of Crumley grandparents (1938)

My earliest childhood memories take place in the small town of Jonesborough, the oldest town in Tennessee. That's where my parents operated a feed store and hatchery. This business, owned by a man named Chapin, was located to the left of the town square. The feed store sold baby chicks, animal food, garden seeds, and small tools used in farming. The large incubator maintained a warm temperature that hatched the eggs into baby chicks in three weeks. Dad worked there for a short time to gain experience before opening his own chick hatchery.

Figure 3. Historic house in Jonesborough that was once a boarding house. Ruth and parents, Glenn and Grace Crumley, lived here for a brief time in the 1930s. (2022)

We lived in one room in a nearby boarding house run by the Broyles family. They provided meals for those who lived there. Built in the 1840s by Dr. Cunningham, a local physician, the house remains today as one of the town's historic sites.[1] The two-story brick house sits between a creek at the front and railroad

---

[1] Russell, Dava Lee, *A Family's Heritage*, Wilco Publishing Company, Jonesborough, Tennessee, 1996.

tracks in back. Imprinted in my memory is the fishpond in the front yard. It's perhaps no coincidence that I find myself tending a fishpond in my backyard today.

Figure 4. Ruth Eleanor Crumley.
(1937)

We moved to Jonesborough when I was about a year old. I have a 1937 picture of me taken in a Jonesborough studio. We stayed there for just one or two chick hatching seasons in the spring.

Both my parents worked in the feed store, and they took me to work with them. Mama said they had to watch me closely so that I wouldn't get into the seed bins and start mixing the seeds together. I must have been an active and inquisitive child!

Another story from Jonesborough is that I got a bottle of Mama's perfume and drank some of it. Mama gave me a dose of castor oil, a foul-tasting remedy given for many childhood illnesses—or it may have been punishment!

Knowing the history of my parents, Glenn Fine Crumley and Marian Grace Thomas Crumley, helps to better understand my childhood.

Glenn Fine Crumley (1911-1994)

Glenn was the oldest of five children born to James Robert and Ida Frances Fine Crumley. They lived in a two-story white frame house at their farm on Weaver Pike, near the intersection with Silver Grove Road, in Sullivan County, Tennessee. (The house remains there today but is no longer owned by the family.) It was a three-generation household that included the Crumley grandparents William and Nannie Crumley and their unmarried daughter Jennie, parents James Robert and Ida Crumley, and children, Glenn, Martha, Mary, Andrew, and James.

Near the house was a general store that the family operated for several years. This store, along with the one-room school (named Triangle), Silver Grove Lutheran Church, and the church parsonage, formed the center of this rural community. The Crumleys were pillars of the church and the community. My grandfather was elected to County Court and served 24 years. Grandmother taught at Triangle School for a few years before she married.

Growing Up

Glenn's dad bought a Model T car that Glenn drove while he went to Bluff City High School because there was no bus transportation. Glenn graduated from high school, but his education did not end there. He was self-educated, reading technical books and figuring out how to build equipment that would be useful on the farm. He could have been an engineer. I believe that my son John inherited some of his grandfather's abilities.

In 1949, *Country Gentleman* magazine featured Glenn in an article titled "He's a Sight for Making Things."[2] The magazine details many of Glenn's accomplishments—building a waterwheel to generate electricity and many labor-saving tools to make farm work easier. With his German ancestry, religious upbringing, and family values, Glenn became a serious, hard-working man who could be very stern, but he usually maintained a dry sense of humor.

Glenn had high expectations for himself and for his family. In the words of his brother James at Glenn's funeral: "He asked a lot of himself. He was never one to make excuses, not one to whine, not one to find others, or the weather, or the circumstances to blame. He would do whatever it took to do what ought to be done as he saw it. He asked a lot of his family.

---

[2] Bloomfield, Howard, "He's a Sight for Making Things," *Country Gentleman*, September 1949, pp. 28-29, 69-70, 72.

He wanted the best for them, and he knew that the best comes only to those who give their best."

Marian Grace Thomas Crumley (1916-2006)

Grace was the eighth of eleven children born to Walter Clyde Thomas and Mary Elizabeth Humphreys Thomas. They lived on a farm in what is now the Holston Valley community of Sullivan County. Life was a struggle for the family. One child died in infancy. When Grace was eight years old, her father died in a car accident.

Just two years later, Grace's 20-year-old sister Edna died. The circumstances of her death brought much sorrow and heartache for the family. It was something we never talked about when I was growing up. Later, when I asked about Edna's death, I was told that she had been murdered, and they never found out who did it. The newspaper account of her death describes Edna as an attractive young woman who was living and working in Bristol. Apparently, she was having an affair with a married man. The coroner ruled her death a suicide, according to the news item.

Grace's oldest sister Anna married, had one child, and divorced. While Anna worked to support herself, her daughter Mary lived with her grandmother.

Grace's mother made the farm and home self-sufficient by growing their food, canning and preserving, and using hand-me-down clothing. She initiated projects such as raising geese so they could make goose feather mattresses. Their cash crop was tobacco, which paid property taxes and bought shoes for the children.

They bartered. If they needed something like flour or kerosene, Grandmother Thomas would send one kid to the store with eggs or possibly a chicken. Granddaughter Mary Dove Nidiffer described her grandmother as a "saint." I agree. I can't imagine how she carried on in these circumstances, and I never heard her say a harsh word during the years I knew her.

Grace wanted to get an education so that she could become a teacher. Through hard work and determination, she became the first in her family to graduate from high school. She had to walk more than a mile to get a ride into Bristol where she attended Bristol Tennessee High School. She knew she could not go to college, so she gave up her goal of becoming a teacher and took a business course to help her get a job.

Grace became a hard-working, resourceful, and determined adult. However, she must have felt insecure and fearful for herself and her family.

Glenn and Grace

I asked Mama how she and Dad had met. She told me she was visiting her sister, Golda Thomas McClelland, who lived on Silver Grove Road, not far from the Crumley home. There had been a death in the McClelland family. One visitor to the home was Mary Crumley, Glenn's sister.

Becoming Independent

Mary went home and told Glenn, "There's a pretty, young Thomas girl you should meet." Shortly thereafter, Glenn asked Oll McClelland, Golda's brother-in-law, to take him for a visit to the Thomas home so he could meet Grace. Thus, their courtship began. Grace was just 16 years old at the time and attending high school. She was indeed a pretty girl, slender and petite, with dark curly hair.

Glenn and Grace were married on August 18, 1934, in the Silver Grove Lutheran Church parsonage. The Reverend Frank L. Roof, who would later be married to Glenn's sister Mary, performed the ceremony. Having the marriage ceremony at the church parsonage was customary in this rural community during the Depression.

Glenn and Grace moved into the Crumley home for a short time as they prepared to make their home at the small farm owned by Glenn's mother on Paddle Creek Road. This property had been in the family since Samuel Millard purchased the land in 1792. Glenn and Grace were the sixth generation of descendants (from Samuel Millard) who would live there.

No one had lived in the house on the property for some time, and it had reverted to a storage barn for tobacco. Glenn and Grace set about making the house livable. This is the house where I was born—no indoor plumbing and no electricity. The outhouse was up the hill a short distance from the house.

Mary Morrell Oliver, a nearby neighbor of Glenn and Grace, told me she would see the young couple walking on a path through the woods, going from their new home to the Crumley home just a couple of miles away. With their first tobacco crop, Glenn and Grace bought a pickup truck. Glenn began figuring out how they would make a living on their 65 acres. Part of his plan led him to Jonesborough, about 30 miles away, where he gained experience in operating a chick hatchery.

Their First Child

I was born on February 13, 1936. My parents were concerned that my delivery would take place during bad weather and the doctor might not make it. The doctor got there, and there were no complications with my birth. They named me Ruth Eleanor, Ruth in honor of Dad's cousin, Ruth Boy, and Eleanor because of Eleanor Roosevelt's prominence at that time.

I have just a few memories of life in the "old house," as Mama called it. I remember lying on the linoleum floor in the dining room and drinking milk from a bottle. When I accidentally pulled the nipple off the bottle, milk spilled all over me and onto the floor. Mama scolded me, and this hurt my feelings. I must have been about two years old.

The original house underwent a couple of additions. There were three bedrooms, a living room, a kitchen, and a dining room. The dining room had a floor door that people could lift to access the cellar below. No closets. There was a long porch on one side of the house. I remember the sweet smell of the blossoms on the mock orange bush near the porch. I've been told, but I don't remember, that I got stung by bumble bees several times. Perhaps I got too close to the blossoms where the bees were.

Mama told me I took her high school class ring and lost it. No one ever found it, and I know it was a loss to her.

I remember we had a German Shepherd dog. A neighbor complained that the dog had killed his sheep, and Dad had to get rid of him. This was my first experience of what can happen to a pet on a farm—farm animals have greater status than any pet.

Another memory is when I was sitting in the pickup truck leaning against the door when Dad opened it, and I fell out. I wasn't injured, but the experience made me more cautious when I was in the truck, both when it was parked and when it was moving.

Figure 5. Ruth Crumley (1939)

GROWING UP

Grandmother Crumley crocheted a coat and cap for me. The dark red coat made me feel special when I wore it. When I had grown taller and the coat was becoming too small, Grandmother crocheted to add a couple of inches to the coat's length.

I liked going to my Crumley grandparents' big house with its two screened porches, one downstairs and one upstairs, that was used as a sleeping porch during the summer. The house underwent several expansions to accommodate the growing family of five children. There was no indoor plumbing or bathroom in the house during my early years. They had an outdoor privy and a potty in each bedroom for nighttime use.

My favorite aunt was Aunt Blanche, Mama's sister. She would take me on overnight visits to Grandmother Thomas's house where she was still living, and I remember the comfort of sinking into a soft feather bed. Aunt Blanche would take me along on her dates with Billy O'Dell whom she later married. We would usually stop at a hamburger drive-in place, and I would get a Coke.

In the early 1940s, TVA took the Thomas home and farm to make way for South Holston Dam. Grandmother Thomas then bought a smaller brick house in Bristol that became a gathering place for the family, including aunts, uncles, and cousins.

BECOMING INDEPENDENT

A New House and a Second Child

Figure 6. House on farm in Sullivan County where Ruth grew up. Built by Glenn Crumley in 1940 at a cost of $2,000.

It is to my parents' credit that they could get established and save money to build a new house in a few years. The house was located a short distance from the old house, with a spring just below that provided a good water supply. Dad built a waterwheel on the creek that ran through the property, and he generated electricity for a while before TVA brought electricity to the area. My parents were getting established in the poultry business.

Dad did most of the work in building the house that had three bedrooms, living room, dining room, kitchen, bath, and basement. He also made a dining room table and chairs and a bed. In later years, he would build more furniture using wood from the farm.

Growing Up

We moved into the house shortly before Claude Eugene Crumley was born on August 21, 1940. Claude was born at home, as I had been. The doctor who delivered Claude was Dr. E.H. Hearst, the rural doctor who delivered many babies, including me, during his career.

In those days, children weren't prepared for the birth of a brother or sister as they are now. I knew nothing about a coming addition to our family. One day, for no particular reason, my parents sent me to stay with my Crumley grandparents. When I came home, they told me I had a baby brother. I thought, or maybe I said, "I would rather have had a sister, but a brother will do."

They named my baby brother Claude for our mother's brother, Claude Thomas. Uncle Claude and Aunt Nell didn't have children at that time, so it must have been a real honor for him to have a namesake.

After being an only child with many doting aunts and uncles, I must have had some feelings about now having to share attention with Claude. Soon after Claude was born, Uncle Claude and Aunt Nell came to visit, bringing a gift for the new baby, but nothing for me. I expressed my hurt feelings, and the next time they came to visit, they brought gifts for both of us.

Claude must have been born with allergies. He had eczema, and one day we found him lying in his bed all covered with blood because he had scratched his body. It was a frightening sight. To keep that from happening again, Mama put socks on his hands.

Claude also had asthma. My parents took him to the hospital emergency room on at least one occasion because of breathing difficulty. As he grew older, his asthma attacks became less severe and less frequent.

Claude grew from a beautiful baby to an adorable little boy with big brown eyes and brown curls. With my own very straight hair, I envied his curls.

A Third Child

Donald Charles Crumley was born four years later, on June 5, 1944, at Bristol Memorial Hospital—the only one of three children to be born in a hospital. It was also a sad time, because my Grandmother Crumley, after several years as an invalid, died on the day Don was born. I remember that friends and family gathered at my grandparents' house to pay their respects to my grandmother, lying in a casket in the living room. Dad took Claude and me to say goodbye to our Grandmother Crumley.

Aunt Blanche came to stay while Mama was in the hospital and for a few days after she came home with the new baby. Don grew into a happy and healthy little boy.

I grew up when the rules were "spare the rod and spoil the child" and "children should be seen and not heard." My parents believed in carrying out these rules. Spanking or whipping with a switch hurt my feelings more than causing physical pain. I remember one spanking during my early years when I was misbehaving in church. I don't remember what I did, but I remember Dad taking me outside and giving me a good spanking. I remember sitting on a stool at my Crumley grandparents' house after church and crying like my heart was breaking.

Don tells me that whenever he got a spanking, he would come running to me because I always took up for him. I remember two childhood accidents involving Don. On a family outing, with the three kids in the back seat, Don opened the door and fell out of the car onto a gravel road. Fortunately, the car was not moving very fast, and his injuries were minor. The second accident occurred when I was helping get supper on the table. As I was carrying a cup of coffee, Don ran into me, and I spilled coffee on his head. He remembers saying "it doesn't hurt," trying to lessen the scolding I was getting. He claims he doesn't have any scars today.

The three of us used a trailer that had wheels in the middle as a seesaw. We would run from one end to the other to make the trailer go up and down. When I got off, the edge of the trailer came down on my big toe. I ran to the house crying, "Get Daddy," thinking he was the one to handle an emergency. There was a lot of blood, and I lost a toenail, but no serious injury. Today, that type of injury would warrant a visit to the hospital emergency room and a tetanus shot.

We were fortunate not to have had any serious accidents or injuries with all the potential dangers that come with farm life. I recall that someone helping Dad build a barn fell and broke his leg.

Becoming Independent

Celebrating Holidays

We celebrated two holidays—Christmas and Easter. Other holidays and birthdays went by largely unnoticed. We went to church on Christmas Eve, and Santa came while we were away. We opened our gifts when we came back home. One year, Santa was still there, and we got to see him and talk to him. Seeing Santa confirmed my belief that Santa was real. Later, I learned this Santa was our Uncle Claude.

We each received two or three gifts at Christmas. I got the usual dolls, paper dolls, coloring books, and books. Dad made a doll bed for me, and I believe my granddaughter Jessica now has it. One Christmas, Don and Claude got an electric train, and another year they got a telescope.

We usually had some fireworks—firecrackers, roman candles, and sparklers—at Christmas. I didn't like firecrackers, but I enjoyed sparklers. Our Christmas tree was always a cedar tree that was cut from the farm. Mama made a fruitcake from vanilla wafer crumbs, cream, maraschino cherries, and nuts. She mixed the ingredients, molded the cake, refrigerated it, and sliced the cake just before serving.

Mama and Dad rarely had gifts for each other, but one year, Dad bought a record player for Mama. He showed us kids where he had hidden it on top of an incubator. I don't know how Mama found it and got her record player before Christmas. She especially liked playing Eddie Arnold music.

We also celebrated Christmas with each of the extended family groups, Crumley and Thomas. Because there were so many of us in the Thomas family, we drew names for gifts. Somehow, Grandmother Thomas had a gift for each grandchild for several years. I liked the Bible stories published in comic book form that she gave me, and I read them over and over.

At Sunday School each child got a brown bag filled with treats—oranges, apples, nuts, and candy. In a family discussion, Dad questioned whether this was necessary. Uncle Haskel answered that without the treat bags, some children would have nothing for Christmas. This statement made me aware that I was fortunate.

Another special Christmas memory was the year a German family, the Gehres, had arrived at our farm. This had come about through Dad's efforts with the Lutheran Church to help displaced German families following World War II. There were three children—Waltraud, Edwin, and Hubert. They spoke little English. On Christmas Eve, we took the family to church. Oh, how their faces glowed when they heard familiar Christmas music. They sang along in German to *Silent Night (Stille Nacht)* and *O Christmas Tree (O Tannenbaum)*. Music can indeed serve as a universal language to bridge many barriers.

Easter was an occasion to get a new outfit. We always had Easter baskets with colored eggs and candy. Easter was a busy time for Mama with the job of dyeing baby chicks that were sold to retail stores in the area. So, she gave me the job of coloring the Easter eggs when I was about 12 years old. Her instructions to me were to "boil the eggs for 10 minutes." I put the eggs in a large pan, covered them with water, and placed the pan on the stove burner. Then I turned on the burner and waited 10 minutes before removing the pan from the heat. By that time, the water had barely begun to boil. I created beautifully colored eggs, but whenever someone dropped an egg, it splattered! That incident became a family joke.

I remember an Easter at Grandmother Thomas's home when it snowed, and my cousins and I hid Easter eggs inside the house. We always had fun in this big house.

More Memories

We grew most of our food on the farm with a garden, chickens and eggs, a milk cow, and hogs. Mama did a lot of canning, including some meat. I remember canned sausage that required several steps. Mama ground the pork and then seasoned it with salt, pepper, and herbs. Next, she sauteed it. The final step was to fill Mason canning jars with the sausage and process them in a large can filled with water.

At hog butchering time, she made what was called liver mush, combining cornmeal with cooked and chopped liver. After refrigerating the liver mush, it became a hard mass that was sliced and fried. These memories help explain the fact that I have never liked liver in any form.

In the late 1940s, frozen food lockers became available in Bristol. These were in large buildings with individual lockers for rent, and we had a locker. Dad would have a cow butchered at a meat processing facility, and then he stored the meat in a locker. When we went to town on Saturday, we would stop at the food locker to get meat for the coming week.

Chicken feed came in flowered cotton sacks. These made very good dishtowels. The sacks were often used to make dresses, and I had a few that someone sewed for me. I thought the dresses were not very pretty.

Mama taught me to do embroidery at about the time that I started school at age 6, and I remember embroidering designs of flowers on pillowcases and dishtowels. I enjoyed my embroidery work, and I was pleased that Mama liked what I did.

I had very straight, coarse hair when curls were in fashion. Mama chose an easy-care hairstyle for me—a boyish bob. I hated it. When I was about 12 years old, she allowed me to get a perm at a beauty shop.

The Morrells, Lena and Porter, who lived on Harrington Hollow Road, were our closest neighbors. Their children, Mary and Eddie, were in their teens by the time I was born. Mary did babysitting and looked after me occasionally. The Morrells had turkeys, and if I went to their house, I was likely to get chased by a big turkey gobbler.

The Cox family lived on the adjacent farm just east of ours. They had four or five children. Jane and Matt were closest to my age, but I saw little of them. Mrs. Cox and Mama became friends, and they would go to PTA meetings together. Mama never learned to drive, but she seemed to get where she wanted to go.

Becoming Independent

After we moved into the new house, the "old house" became a tenant house for several years. Dad had help from tenant farmers until Don and Claude were old enough to take over these responsibilities.

We had a large extended family with Grandpa Crumley and Grandma Thomas, aunts and uncles, nine first cousins from the Crumley side and fourteen from the Thomas side. We saw them on frequent Sunday afternoon visits at the grandparents' homes. On Dad's side of the family, Aunt Mary and Uncle Frank were the only ones who lived away from the Bristol area. I always looked forward to seeing my cousin Ina Lee when they came to visit. Mama's sister Verna, who didn't have children, lived in Norfolk, and she came back to visit from time to time.

It was customary to just drop in for family visits. This practice probably began before everyone had telephones, but it continued long after that time. Annette Crumley said that Grandpa would come to visit them in Oak Ridge in the 1950s without calling in advance. One time, Grandpa arrived just as they were packing the car to go on a brief trip.

When Grandma Thomas sold her farm, she gave each of her children a cash gift. Mama used some of this money to buy a new electric stove. She had this appliance about a week when I dropped a plate that chipped the porcelain from a corner of the stove as I was cleaning up the kitchen after supper. Dad managed to cover the chip with a porcelain repair, but it was never like new. I felt like I had ruined it. My parents cautioned me to be more careful in the kitchen, but they didn't punish me.

Another accident—Dad's—occurred when Dad was painting a bedroom and spilled a bucket of blue paint in the middle of the bed. My parents cleaned up the mess, but the spilled paint ruined the bedding. Mama never asked him to paint again; she would hire someone to do it.

My parents seldom argued. However, I remember one argument in which Mama complained that all the money was going into the farm and little for the house. Dad told her to buy whatever she wanted for the house; she didn't need to get his approval. From then on, I believe she did just that. She was very supportive of whatever Dad wanted, including photography equipment and the costs of flying a plane.

Dad installed an alarm inside the house to alert us during the night if there was a problem with the incubators—a power failure or a fluctuation in temperature. The alarm seemed to go off a lot. One or both parents would get up to investigate and correct the problem. If we had a power failure, Dad would start the generator.

One winter, a company truck driver delivered a new incubator. As the incubator was being unloaded and set up, it began snowing, and so Dad decided the driver should stay the night. He had supper with us, and I gave him my bedroom. I slept on the living room sofa.

The first phone I remember was a crank phone on the wall. We had a party line that served about a dozen families. If you wanted to call someone on your line, you cranked their specific ring. Ours was a long and three shorts. And we heard everyone else's ring, too. Sometimes you could tell that someone on the line was listening. If you wanted to call someone not on your line, you cranked the phone to get the operator and gave her the number you wanted. She then rang the number for you. It was in the late 1940s that we went from crank to dial phones. Who would have imagined the smart phones we have today!

We listened to the radio a lot—everything from music, evangelists, weather, news, to programs such as *Inner Sanctum, The Shadow,* and *The Aldrich Family*. The first television set I saw was at a classmate's house around 1949. It had a small screen (about 7 inches), and the black-and-white picture was "snowy." The one available TV station was some distance away in Charlotte, North Carolina. My parents got a TV a couple of years later when a station opened in nearby Johnson City. It was a big, bulky set, and we had a large antenna outside. We watched programs like *Gunsmoke, I Love Lucy,* and *Lawrence Welk*.

I was a sensitive child when it came to farm animals. I didn't like hog butchering time, seeing a chicken's head chopped off, or disposing of the baby roosters. We were hatching baby chicks in incubators for producing hens that would lay eggs. Chick sex was determined by George Fuji, a Japanese man who came from Knoxville. (This was a specialty taught and promoted by the Japanese following World War II.) We had no use for the roosters, so we put them in barrels and drowned them. Then we plowed them into the fields to fertilize the soil.

Dad had no use for horses, because he had spent too much time in his youth behind a horse and plow. We never had a horse on the farm. Dad bought an Allis Chalmers tractor that Uncle Jim remembered driving to the farm after he and Dad picked it up in Johnson City.

The farm was not a good place for pets, especially dogs. Stray dogs would show up from time to time. By the time I got attached to one, it was either scaring or killing the chickens on the outdoor range, and it was done away with. Later, we had a collie named Shep, and he became our family pet.

Cats were usually around as outdoor pets. I remember one litter of three cats. I named them Tiger, Big Boy, and Pretty Face. Whenever I was feeling sad or hurt, I would find these cats to get comfort from petting them and hearing them purr.

One of my chores, when I was about 10 years old, was to go into the pasture and bring Blackie, the milk cow, to the barn where Mama milked her. I never learned to milk a cow. Once, when I had Blackie in the barn and we were waiting for Mama, I tried unsuccessfully to do the milking. I got a scolding because I had upset Blackie, and then she wouldn't "give her milk" when Mama tried milking her. I never tried milking again. Blackie was gentle, but very protective when she had a calf.

Uncle Haskel gave me a canary that I named Bobby. He lived in a cage that we kept inside the house. I fed Bobby and gave him water. Unfortunately, one day when Mama and I were outside cleaning the cage, Bobby got away, never to be seen again. This memory stuck with me as an adult, and I got another canary. When I told Uncle Haskel that I had a canary, he didn't remember that he had given me one. He said, "If I did, I don't want it back."

Becoming Independent

Hummingbirds fascinated me because they were so tiny and could fly so fast. I asked Mama if I could keep one if I caught it. She must have known that was an easy promise to make and said "yes." I never caught one, but it was not because I didn't try.

Uncle Claude gave us a rabbit that didn't make a very good pet. It didn't react to our attention like a dog or cat would. We kept the rabbit in an outdoor storage shed, and we had the responsibility of giving it food and water. It must have gotten out of the shed and run away to be eaten by a predator.

One summer, when the corn crib was empty, Mama made it into a playhouse for me. I brought my dolls, some toys, and a few household items. I had fun. However, whenever it rained, something always got wet because the sides of the crib were wire mesh.

An amusing incident occurred when Dad and some other men were working at the barn. Dad called to me to bring them some "ice water." I heard "fly swatter" and that's what I took to the barn. There were big horse flies around the barn, so it seemed logical to me that a fly swatter was what they needed.

Aunt Martha and Uncle Haskel took Don, Claude, and me, along with their children Bobby and Mary Ellen, on a one-day train trip to Greeneville, Tennessee. Riding a train was an exciting thing to do. In Greeneville, we visited Aunt Mary and Uncle Frank and our cousins, Ina Lee and David. Aunt Mary made a salad—orange Jello with grated carrots, pineapple, and chopped pecans. I have made it a few times since.

Growing Up

A year or two during the polio scare, we stayed home more closely rather than risk being exposed. And there was tuberculosis. Mama and I visited a family on Harrington Hollow Road. We took a gift of toiletries to the teenage daughter who was being admitted to the tuberculosis sanitarium in Knoxville.

Dad had always wanted to fly a plane. He studied for his license in ground school during the evening at an airport near Bristol. Following ground school, Dad soloed, and after a specified number of hours of flying, he passed the test and got his license. We began spending our Sunday afternoons at the airport.

When Dad was in ground school, this gave Mama, Claude, Don, and me time to go to a movie in Bristol. Dad would drop us off and pick us up after his class. We never timed it right to get there at the beginning of a movie.

I remember a traumatic incident that occurred during a movie. When we got there, we didn't find four seats together. Mama, Don, and Claude sat together in the center section. I found a seat a few rows further back and to the left. A young man, probably in his teens, sat down beside me. He began putting his hands on me while I was telling him to stop and pushing him away. After a few minutes, a woman employee of the theater came and ordered him to leave. She told me if this ever happened again, to come for help right away. I can't explain why I didn't leave my seat, scream, or ask for help. It must have been that I was afraid of calling attention to myself and felt I was somehow to blame. This happened when I was about 11 or 12 years old. I never told anyone about this traumatic incident.

As I grew into my teen years, I felt that my parents' rules were too strict. One rule was that they did not permit me to wear shorts, except for gym class in school, or jeans. This rule related to their ideas about appropriate attire for women and girls.

Both parents were ready to criticize and slow to praise. This applied not only to their children, but to others as well. Neither parent was affectionate.

On the positive side, my parents were supportive of my 4-H projects. Dad took many pictures for my 4-H record book. Dad had gotten into photography as a hobby and had his own darkroom in the basement.

Mama was easily upset, and I felt she took it out on me. I got blamed for whatever went wrong just because I was there. She had several health problems over the years that must have caused her to be irritable. I never knew until Don's wife Emily told me that Mama had suffered a miscarriage. I could never confide in Mama, and evidently she could not confide in me.

Dad was stern, but easier going. I remember an incident when I was putting food on the table, and I spilled some beans. Dad said, "It's not worth crying over spilled milk—or spilled beans!"

I married George Paire, whom I met in high school, against my parents' wishes, and they informed me that their farm and property would go to Don and Claude. I agreed that this was what they should do, since Don and Claude stayed on the farm.

Growing Up

After my marriage, I made a special effort to stay in contact with my parents, and George remained on friendly terms with them. They gave us financial gifts from time to time that helped greatly. Mama always sent me a birthday card with a check.

I know my actions in defying my parents' wishes made it harder for my brothers. Claude earned a degree from King College near Bristol while he was also working on the farm. Claude told me that in addition to discouraging him from going to college, Dad made it hard for him to go to college. I'm sure Dad complained about my going to college and dropping out to get married. He felt that sending me to college had been a waste.

It was not until the last few years that I have come to understand what made my parents as they were. They wanted to protect me. And they didn't want me to cause them shame and sorrow like Mama's sister Edna had caused her family. I know they wanted the best for me as they saw it. I've made peace with the past.

In 1992, Dad handed me a letter from the Sullivan County Historical Society asking for submissions of family histories. He said, "Here, you're the only one who can do this." This made me realize I had earned his approval. I'm grateful that the Historical Society published the book with my story of the Glenn Crumley family a few months before Dad's death in 1994.[3]

---

[3] Johnson, Ruth C., "Glenn Crumley Family," *Families and History of Sullivan County, Tennessee, Volume One, 1779-1992*, Holston Territory Genealogical Society, Wadsworth Publishing, 1992.

BECOMING INDEPENDENT

In 2003, Mama suffered a heart attack and needed round-the-clock care for the remaining three years of her life. Don, Emily (Don's wife), and Claude made the sacrifices necessary to care for her at home. They hired a caregiver for weekdays. Emily checked on her when she got home from work, and Don and Claude took turns spending the night with her. I came up about one weekend a month to give them a much-needed break. Mama became more mellow and easy-going those last three years, and that made it easier to care for her.

Near the time of Mama's 90th birthday, I came up for the weekend. When I said goodbye, I told Mama that she had been a good mother and I loved her. She said, "I love you, too." That was the only time either of us had ever spoken these words. Three days later, she died. She had lived for 90 years and one week.

Reflections

The life we had when I was growing up has largely disappeared. It was a stable family life for me with two parents and the fact that we lived in the same community all those years. I benefitted from this stability and from having a large extended family. I was fortunate to have known three of my grandparents. We weren't wealthy, but we always had enough. From my parents, I learned the value of working hard and being frugal. My parents saved money to buy what they wanted rather than going into debt.

Growing Up

Mama became my first role model in what women can accomplish. She was always a full partner with Dad in operating the farm, using the bookkeeping and typing skills she learned in high school. As a community leader, she served as president of the Weavers PTA and a member of the Sullivan County Agricultural Extension Committee.

Mama taught me to find pleasure and beauty in making a home. From her, I learned to enjoy growing flowers and using them in arrangements for church. It is to her credit that I am now part of a group that arranges altar flowers for church.

One thing I learned from Dad was to follow my dreams. He made his dream of flying a plane a reality. I would later follow my dreams of education and travel. Dad's interest in genealogy and preserving our family history led me to pursue this interest. I researched and documented our Crumley ancestors for the First Families of Tennessee project of the East Tennessee Historical Society. And Dad inspired me to write my memoir.

I'm grateful to have Don and Claude as my brothers. We have fond memories of our shared life experiences, and they remain my friends today. Their wives, Emily and Mary Alice, are much loved and appreciated.

Figure 7. Ruth with brothers Claude and Don, who now operate the family farm. (2020)

Marriage

Traditions and Expectations

I grew up when most, if not all, girls expected to get married. People saw getting a college education as a way to prepare to become a better homemaker, wife, and mother. And some thought that girls went to college to find a husband. Traditionally, society viewed a career like teaching as a temporary pursuit that women often abandoned when they got married or started a family.

Many teenage girls started a hope chest of household items they would need when they married. I didn't have a hope chest, but I began sets of china and sterling silver with urging from Mama. Girls thought of china and silver as luxury items that would be nice to have.

Cohabiting couples or having a baby outside of marriage were practices not condoned, if not considered sinful. People rarely discussed same-sex relationships except in off-color jokes.

Most women did not leave home until they married. There were several spinsters (or old maids, as they were called) in our community. Some of them were teachers, while others had no career other than helping out in homes of their parents. I sometimes feared that this could happen to me.

George Edgar Paire (Married 1956-1968)

Figure 8. George Paire in 1953, the year he entered Bluff City High School.

George Paire came to Bluff City High School, as a transfer from Bristol Tennessee High School, in 1953. He attracted attention with his good looks and clothes that differed from the typical country-boy style. No blue jeans for George.

The first time George and I got together was when the Bluff City High School Glee Club participated in an event in Blountville. We rode a bus from Bluff City to Blountville. When we returned to Bluff City that evening, George took me home in his dad's car.

Becoming Independent

Gradually, we developed a relationship that continued through our senior year. We went together to school social events, church activities, and movies. George gave me his class ring, and we considered ourselves "going steady."

George wrote in my high school yearbook:

> Dear Ruth,
> As time goes by and people recall their youth, some things they are happy about and others they regret. Some things I am happy about, others I regret. I hope you will have pleasant memories about me as I will of you. So, I say this to you—here's to the girl that's good and pure, here's to the girl that's true, here's to the girl that stole my heart. In other words, Ruth, here's to you. May you have a little place in your heart for me, as I will always have for you.
> Love you now and forever,
> George E. Paire

I grew fond of George's family—parents Rob and Pauline and his brothers, Robert Jr. (Sonny) and Glenn (Zeke). They had a warmth and affection that we lacked in my family.

I had plans to go to the University of Tennessee in Knoxville, while George would follow his brother Sonny at East Tennessee State College (now University) in Johnson City. George's dream was to become a lawyer. I wanted to be a 4-H agent with the Agricultural Extension Service.

Marriage

During that first year in college, George and I saw each other on occasional weekends when he would come to Knoxville, or I would go home. I came to enjoy the freedom and independence of being away from home. I managed my time to include study, work, and some social activities.

By the time George and I began the second year of college, we were talking about getting married. The plan was that George would go to Michigan and get a job in the auto industry and work a few months to save some money, and I would finish the school year at UT. We would then get married during the summer and move to Knoxville where we would both attend UT and support ourselves by working part time.

During Thanksgiving vacation, we talked with my parents about our plans. My parents were strongly opposed to this plan and refused to finance the remainder of my school year (winter and spring quarters) at UT. I took final exams to complete the fall quarter and returned to my parents' home in Bristol. Subsequently, George went to Flint, Michigan, and I got a job at Inter-Mountain Telephone Company in Bristol.

George returned from Michigan in May. We were both 20 years old, and parents' signatures were required to get a marriage license in Sullivan County. My parents would probably have refused to sign. Therefore, we got our marriage license in nearby Carter County where the required age was 18. George's mother Pauline arranged with The Reverend Robert Parsons, pastor of Bluff City Methodist Church, to perform the ceremony at a church in Elizabethton (in Carter County). George's parents and brothers attended the ceremony on May 18, 1956. No one from my family attended.

George and I had a weekend honeymoon in Gatlinburg. Then it was off to Knoxville in search of a place to live. We found a tiny apartment near the college campus. The apartment at 1203 Laurel Avenue, Apartment 5, had a sleeping/living area, a small kitchen, bath, and closet and rented for $55 a month. It was in a beautiful old house that would later be in the movie based on James Agee's autobiographical book, *Death in the Family*.

George found a summer job selling vacuum cleaners at Sears. I went to work at Tennessee Valley Bank and became our support for George to go to college in the fall. George would take me to work in the morning, and I would ride the bus home in the afternoon. On Fridays, after I got off from work around 7 p.m., George would pick me up and we would go grocery shopping. We spent about $10 a week on groceries. On Saturdays, I would clean the apartment, do some baking, and do laundry. I took our clothes to a laundromat a block away and picked them up after they had been washed. I would hang them to dry on the clotheslines in our yard.

By the time George began the fall term at UT, it was obvious there was no room for books and studying in our small apartment. George located a basement apartment at 401 Mimosa Avenue, just across the Tennessee River. When I came home from work, I could get off the bus at either Henley Street or Gay Street and walk across the bridge. Our apartment house was near the Kern Bakery.

Marriage

The apartment had three rooms with a bath and large closet, and we had access to a garage. I remember there were bars on the windows. Rent was $50 a month. Our apartment was comfortable, and I would have been content to stay, but George found another place for us.

The Neely family had a small two-room house in their backyard at 2216 Highland Avenue, near the UT campus. We rented it for $35 a month. The bath facilities were inconvenient. You had to walk through the shower space to get to the toilet. Hand washing, brushing teeth, etc. had to be done at the kitchen sink. Mama gave us her old wringer clothes washer. I hung washed clothes on outside lines to dry.

We adopted an orange cat and named him Thomas. George trained him to be an outdoor cat. He built a perch for Thomas outside a window and beneath the overhang of the house. We couldn't take Thomas with us when we moved to Sutherland Village, the UT apartments on Sutherland Avenue, so we gave him to the Neely family.

In those days, we didn't have much money or time for recreation. We went to an occasional movie and had a meal at a restaurant. I remember going to the Tennessean restaurant, a popular place for students, on Cumberland Avenue. For outdoor activities, we would go to nearby Tyson Park and to Big Ridge State Park. We made occasional weekend visits back to Bristol where we stayed with George's parents, and we also visited my family.

Becoming Independent

George decided we could donate blood to get some extra money. I remember the payment amount being $20. So, we went on a Saturday to give blood. They took his blood, but they wouldn't take mine because my weight was below the 110-pound minimum requirement for blood donors.

At about the same time that we moved to the little house, George applied for UT married student housing at Sutherland Village on Sutherland Avenue, just a few miles from the UT campus. UT had converted Army barracks to housing for returning veterans after World War II. We moved there in 1957, going from a one-bedroom apartment, Number 86, to a two-bedroom, Number 93, after son John was born. Rent was $23 a month for the one-bedroom unit and $26 for the two-bedroom.

We had a kerosene heater in the living room and a kerosene cooking stove and a kerosene water heater in the kitchen. Behind the apartment was a drum for kerosene, and we used a can to carry kerosene inside. The kerosene created an odor and smoke that blackened the walls. There was one 15-amp electric circuit in each apartment. We had a portable electric heater, an electric frying pan, and a clothes washer, so we had to be careful and not turn on more than one at a time or it would blow a fuse. We went through a lot of fuses!

Despite these inconveniences, we were happy to get into student housing, and we enjoyed getting to know other couples who lived there. The situation for most couples was that the husband was attending college under the GI bill and the wife had a job. Some women with children stayed at home, and they were likely to supplement family income by caring for children of working mothers.

George was a UT student and had plans to go to law school. At the time I became pregnant, George got a job in the business office at the University of Tennessee Hospital. He went to work around 4 p.m. and worked about four hours each weekday and usually worked on weekends.

George's brother Sonny was in the Army and managed on his small salary to send George $50 a month to help with his college expenses. While stationed in Texas, he met Jane Warren, and they were married in 1959. After Sonny got out of the Army, they came to Knoxville and got an apartment near ours in Sutherland Village. The plan was that Sonny would get a master's degree at UT. When Jane couldn't find a job in her field of occupational therapy; they returned to Texas. I enjoyed their company during the short time they were in Knoxville.

I remember the time we spent in Sutherland Village as the best years of our marriage. We had friends there, the birth of a child, and George earned both undergraduate and law degrees. During this time, I worked at Tennessee Valley Bank and the University of Tennessee. Wanda and Earl Cole lived near us, and Wanda took care of son John for several years when I was working. We were fortunate to have her.

I had not learned to drive and knew that I would soon need to be driving. Near the time that George would get his law degree, I hired an instructor and learned to drive our VW Beetle.

Becoming Independent

After George earned his law degree in 1962, he got a job with State Farm as an insurance adjuster, and he had to be away for one month of training. We were still living in Sutherland Village and, thus, would be ineligible for UT student housing. During George's absence, I was looking at newspaper ads and found a house at 1601 Duncan Road, off Northshore Drive.

After getting an agreement from George by phone, I rented the house and made the move. George's parents came for the weekend to help. It was a four-room house in a beautiful neighborhood. I remember the rent as $50 a month. There was a garage, but they had filled it with junk. A nice older couple, Hut and Mamie, lived across the street. I adopted a small black puppy that someone brought to my office at UT, and we named her Nancy. Soon George would get a second dog, a boxer that he named Debo.

John went to kindergarten at Bearden Methodist Church. Knoxville public schools did not offer kindergarten. His teacher, Mrs. Venable, was a kind and caring person who told me how smart John was and how well he was doing.

I returned to UT, as we had planned, to finish my degree. However, after I had been a student for one quarter, George wanted to leave his job and get started in law practice. I gave up my studies and found a job at Oak Ridge Institute of Nuclear Studies. My education would have to wait.

After being in the Duncan Road house for a few months, our landlord asked us to leave because he wanted to move his family into the house. The city of Knoxville had annexed the house where he lived, and he didn't want to pay city taxes. The house on Duncan Road was in Knox County, not in Knoxville city limits.

George and I then bought a house at 3970 Greenleaf Avenue for $7,500. These modest houses, located east of West High School, had been built after World War II. This two-bedroom, one-bath house was just the right size and a convenient location for us. We took our two dogs with us.

John began the first grade at Sequoyah Elementary School. Things didn't go well for him. I took John to see Dr. Stiles, his pediatrician, to check for any physical problem that was causing difficulty. Dr. Stiles asked the name of his teacher (I can't remember her name). When I told him, Dr. Stiles replied, "she's the problem." His own children had been in this teacher's class, so he knew what she was like.

Another problem was transportation for John from school to his sitter's house. Our solution was to have a taxi pick him up at school and take him to the home of his sitter. This solution created some problems—one day the taxi didn't show up, and John walked home crossing a heavy traffic area on Kingston Pike.

We enrolled John in Thaxton School, a private school next to the UT campus, when he entered the second grade. He did much better with the change in schools. Thaxton offered after-school care, so I would pick up John after I got off from work. John finished the school year in the second grade at Thaxton. In the fall, he entered third grade at Farragut Elementary School.

Becoming Independent

Soon after George entered law practice, he began spending more time away from home. Sometimes, he had an excuse; other times, he did not even attempt to offer one. There were times when he did not come home at night.

On a Sunday afternoon drive, we went to Sonja Drive near Concord (now Farragut). There we saw a few new houses. The one that caught our attention was at 11001 Sonja Drive, and we bought it a few weeks later for $17,500. We moved there in 1965.

It was good to move into a brand-new house with a beautiful view of the Smoky Mountains from our front windows. At the back of our house was a wooded area. Having the house gave me hope George would succeed as an attorney and our marriage would survive.

George got a German Shepherd that he named Munich. We called her Munnie. After Munnie had given birth to two litters of pups, we took her to the vet to be spayed. She died during surgery. Sometime later, we lost our little black dog Nancy. During a visit to the Crumley farm in Bristol, she encountered an electric fence. She took off running and never came back. We searched but didn't find her. Losing a pet was almost like losing a member of the family, and we grieved for them.

Our marriage didn't survive. George left me in 1968, and we divorced in June of that year. George agreed I should keep the house (and the mortgage), have custody of John, and he would pay $100 a month in child support. In September (just three months after our divorce), he married Harriett, who had been one of his clients.

Marriage

I experienced a range of emotions—sorrow that I had loved and lost, anger that I had spent 12 years helping George get his education and setting up law practice, and relief in knowing that divorce was necessary.

In March 1969, I resumed my education at UT, financed through a gift from my parents, a scholarship, and a student loan. George voluntarily increased the child support payment to $150 a month.

Years later, George married Gale, and his life became more stable. He established a good relationship with John, and I overcame any animosity that I may have had. I met George and Gale at John's 50th birthday celebration in 2008. Sadly, a drunk driver hit and killed George in 2020. Gale, who was injured in the accident, died sometime later.

Figure 9. George Paire with son John at John's 50th birthday party. (2008)

Robert William Johnson (Married 1971-1995)

Figure 10. Robert William (Bill) Johnson. (1990)

Sandra Williams was one of my coworkers at Oak Ridge Institute of Nuclear Students; she left for a job at Y-12. After my divorce, she introduced me to Bill Johnson, who worked in the Y-12 Development Division as a chemist. Later, in referring to this introduction, Bill said, "It pays to be nice to the secretaries."

Bill had grown up in Wisconsin and served in the Navy near the end of World War II. Recently, he went through a divorce after 20 years of marriage and obtained custody of the two children, Gwen and Peter. When we met, I was 32 and Bill was 43. We were aware of the age difference but thought it was not important.

Marriage

At the time we met, I was more interested in completing my education than getting married. Bill understood this and offered me much encouragement. In 1970, I earned my bachelor's degree, and in 1971 I earned a master's degree. It had taken me 16 years to get the bachelor's degree!

My biggest concern about getting married involved the three children. I knew it would be hard to blend a family consisting of a 12-year-old, a 17-year-old, and a 19-year-old, each with their unique personalities, needs, and preferences. And I felt too young to be a mother to Gwen and Peter. Gwen was already in college, and Peter had one more year of high school when Bill and I were married in 1971.

We were married by The Reverend J. Monroe Ball at Concord Methodist Church on June 10, 1971. In addition to the minister and organist, our three children and one of Gwen's friends attended. Bill and I had a brief honeymoon at Fontana Village in North Carolina.

Then began the task of combining two households. Bill and I had bought a house in Oak Ridge at 105 Adelphi Road. For a brief time, we owned three houses. Fortunately, it turned out to be easy to sell my house in Concord and for Bill to sell his house in Oak Ridge.

The move to the new house also involved pets. Gwen had a cat named Thomas, and John had a dog named Mollie. Soon after the move, Thomas disappeared. He must have decided he didn't like sharing the new house with a dog, so he tried to find his way back to his old house. Our attempts to find him were unsuccessful.

Figure 11. Bill and Ruth bought this Oak Ridge house in 1971. Ruth still lives here today. (2024)

Mollie was a long-time companion for John and for Bill and me after John had left home. It was hard to constrain her to our own yard since she had been free to roam when she lived in Concord. She once disappeared over the weekend when there had been a Walk for Mankind event. We figured she had joined the walk, and we found her at the animal shelter on Monday. It took us a long time to clean her up and remove the ticks.

Marriage

My fears about blending the family turned out to be warranted. Gwen and Peter were used to their own ways and little in the way of rules from Bill. John told me years later that he regretted not giving Bill the respect he should have. And I believe Bill did not provide the guidance John needed.

Peter and his friends were coming and going from our house at all hours of the night. Peter was highly intelligent and, like his dad, was always busy working on an electronics project. He entered the Science Fair and won first place in the regional competition.

Gwen returned to Columbia University in New York but came back home during her junior year because of the onset of mental illness. She completed her college degree requirements at UT, and we helped her move to her own apartment. She married, but the marriage didn't last. Gwen's problems continued to be a responsibility for Bill and me through the years and for me following Bill's death.

I had the pleasure of getting to know Gene and Ruth Johnson, Bill's brother and sister-in-law, who lived in Lincoln, Nebraska. They visited us in Oak Ridge, and we visited them in Nebraska. Gene was head librarian at the University of Nebraska, and Ruth was a violinist who played with several groups. She was also music director at her church.

I was also fond of Bill's sister Edith Cross, who lived in Milwaukee. Edith had been a high school math teacher. Following her husband's death, she moved to Lincoln to be near Ruth and Gene.

Becoming Independent

In 1973, I attended a meeting of the American Home Economics Association in Los Angeles. Bill joined me after the meeting, and we rented a car to travel from LA to Portland, Oregon. We spent some time in San Francisco and had visits with Bill's friends. Also, in Lodi near San Francisco, we visited the Gehres family, the German refugees that my parents had sponsored in coming to this country.

In Lincoln City, Oregon, we visited Fritz Johnson, Bill's brother. It seems Fritz's life had been a series of problems. Later, when we learned Fritz was being released from an alcohol treatment program and had nowhere to go, we invited him to come to Oak Ridge. Here he found a job, only to revert to drinking again. He left Oak Ridge and eventually ended up in San Francisco, where he remained until his death.

Bill and I had the opportunity for other travels when we could drive. As a matter of principle, Bill refused to fly after President Reagan fired the air traffic controllers. Bill encouraged me to travel without him. In 1977, I went with an Oak Ridge group on a trip to Europe, and in 1989, I joined a People-to-People group going to the Soviet Union.

Once John was married and had a family, Bill and I frequently met them for a weekend at some half-way point on Skyline Drive or the Blue Ridge Parkway. Also, grandchildren (John's children) Jessica, Crystal, and their brother Clinton would spend a couple of weeks in the summer with us. Bill was a good grandfather, and we shared fun times together. Bill was also grandfather to David and Laura, Peter's children, and we saw them occasionally.

When I wanted to return to UT for graduate study, Bill was most supportive. I could not have earned a PhD without his assistance and encouragement.

The year 1992 was the first in a series of four years that brought sad events. Janice, John's wife, died in a car accident. Her funeral and burial were in Greensboro, North Carolina, where other members of her family were buried. Jane and Sonny, who were then living in Greensboro, invited Bill and me to stay with them. This renewed my relationship with the Paire family, and we kept in touch thereafter.

Bill's illness came on suddenly in September 1993. He had gone to work despite feeling unwell. We decided to go ahead and visit Gwen in Nashville and my niece Sylvia and her family in Clarksville. When Bill began feeling worse, we headed back to Oak Ridge with me driving. The next day, a Sunday, Bill observed his swollen ankles, a symptom of congestive heart failure, and I took him to the hospital emergency room.

Our family doctor immediately called a cardiologist and a pulmonologist. This team of doctors concluded Bill had suffered both a heart attack and a viral infection in his lungs. He was in critical condition, and the doctors urged me to call in family members. Gene and Ruth came from Nebraska, and Peter was living here in Oak Ridge. We informed Gwen, who was in Nashville, but we did not bring her to Oak Ridge. Our minister, Reverend Boyd Carter, provided great support to us.

Becoming Independent

I resigned from my teaching job at Pellissippi State so that I could care for Bill.

Bill came home in November with regular visits from a physical therapist and a nurse. Soon he could go to the cardiopulmonary rehab program at Methodist Medical Center. He was on oxygen during this time. Throughout his illness, Bill maintained an optimistic spirit and outlook.

Bill's friend and co-worker, Paul Tinnel, visited regularly and would stay with Bill when I needed to go out.

In June 1994, Ruth and Gene and Bill's cousin Helen were visiting us when my dad died unexpectedly. Their help in caring for Bill made it possible for me to go to the funeral in Bristol.

I had a surprise 70th birthday dinner for Bill at the Garden Plaza hotel. Attending were Kathleen and Nelson Stephens and Clara and Al Chambles, who became friends with Bill during their civil rights activities.

In April 1995, Bill experienced a second cardio event, and I got him to Methodist Medical Center. After treatment and consultation with doctors, Bill and I decided for him to have heart bypass surgery. He never recovered. I remember walking down the hallway one evening after visiting Bill in the ICU along with Dr. Parrish, one of Bill's doctors. He said to me, "We don't know what the outcome is going to be." I replied, "I know all that can be done has been done." Dr. Parrish replied, "Now it's in God's hands."

On Thursday evening, May 11, as I was leaving, one of the ICU nurses followed me into the hallway. She told me to be prepared to decide about turning off life support systems. I asked her if there was any hope for Bill's recovery. She said, "No, I've seen too many cases like this; he is not going to get better."

On Saturday morning, May 13 around 6 a.m., one of Bill's doctors called and asked me to come in. When I got there, I asked, "Is it time to let him go?" The answer was "Yes." At Bill's bedside, I held his hand and told him it was all right to go. I remembered a few words from Psalm 23 and recited them. Bill died peacefully.

The hospital staff volunteered to make calls for me, and they called Peter, Bill's son, and Jenny Rule, my friend and neighbor. Soon Jenny, Peter, and Linda, Peter's wife, arrived. Jenny invited us to come to her house, where she cooked breakfast for us. What a thoughtful gesture! Then began the task of notifying other family members and making funeral arrangements. Soon, my son John, granddaughters Jessica and Crystal, my mother, and Ruth and Gene arrived. Friends Martha Larsen and Elizabeth Sworski were very helpful.

My uncle Jim Crumley had already planned a trip to East Tennessee, and I asked him to read the scripture at the funeral. Ruth played the violin, and Al Chambles read his tribute to Bill. Aunt Annette Crumley, Aunt Mary Roof, and Uncle Clyde and Aunt Gerry Thomas from Atlanta were at the funeral.

The inscription I chose for Bill's grave marker at Oak Ridge Memorial Park reads "A man with a gentle spirit, committed to justice and peace." I believe these words describe his personality, as well as his life's work. Bill's commitment to justice led him to become active in the civil rights movement, and he believed that his work in weapons development helped maintain peace.

Edwin Douglas Smiley (Married 1998-2022)

Figure 12. Doug and Ruth on a hike at Big South Fork National River and Recreation Area. (2013)

Doug and I met through his newspaper ad looking for companionship in September 1997. I responded to his ad with a telephone call. We discovered we had a mutual interest in hiking, and we arranged to meet at the University of Tennessee

Arboretum in Oak Ridge. Doug brought along some photos he had taken at the Arboretum, and I brought photos from my recent trip to Alaska.

I learned Doug had owned and operated a black-and-white photo lab in Knoxville for several years. His clients included some of Knoxville's best-known photographers. Doug was also an accomplished photographer and had won recognition in several shows.

Doug had been divorced for 14 years and had no children. I'm seven years older than Doug, but that didn't matter to either of us.

In February 1998, we adopted a black cat and named her Samantha. Samantha was about 6 months old, and she became a member of our family until her death in 2013.

Doug and I were married on August 2, 1998, in our backyard gazebo. The Reverend Boyd Carter performed the ceremony, with Susan Carter as a witness. Barry Seaton, one of Doug's clients, took photos. Following the ceremony, we had a reception in our home attended by friends and family.

Doug relocated his business to our house. We converted a bedroom into a darkroom and made office space for Doug in the existing office that I used. This took some time and effort. Also, Doug had to drive to Knoxville for pickup and delivery of his work.

Doug encouraged my interest in photography. Both of us had entries accepted in the Oak Ridge Art Center's Open Shows. Doug got me started in hand painting black and white photos.

He printed the photos on special paper, and I painted them. I took special photos of my nieces' children, along with a few scenes. In 2013, I had a photo accepted by Thrivent Financial for their calendar.

Figure 13. Photo by Ruth Johnson Smiley, selected by Thrivent Financial for their 2013 calendar. Photo portrays the hymn, "When Morning Gilds the Sky."

Doug and I began spending winter vacations in Florida—first in Indian Shores and near Sarasota on the Gulf coast. Then we discovered the Florida Panhandle—St. George Island and Indian Pass. The scenery and the mild weather in this less-developed area attracted us. Storms concerned us, but fortunately there were only minor ones when we were there.

We also visited Jekyll Island and Tybee Island in Georgia.

Kite flying became one of my interests during beach vacations, and I now have a collection of about 20 kites. Doug enjoyed stargazing at the beach and was always hoping for clear, dark skies. The best locations were those where he could set up his telescope on the deck of our rental house.

We took our cat Samantha with us for several years. I tried unsuccessfully to teach her to go for walks on the beach attached to a harness and leash. I soon gave up.

Figure 14. Arbor in our backyard. (2021)

The wood in our gazebo gradually deteriorated. At the point when we realized it had to go, I was ready to give up both the gazebo and fishpond. But Doug convinced me it was worth saving. We replaced the gazebo with an arbor which works well. After some work on the rocks around the fishpond, it has required minimal maintenance. The problem now is keeping falling leaves and pine needles off the pond.

Figure 15. Fishpond in our backyard. (2000)

Doug and I enjoyed the wildlife in our backyard, although we didn't like the damage they did to our plants. Doug kept the bird bath filled with water, and we watched many birds year-round. I especially enjoyed feeding the hummingbirds. We

Marriage

compiled a photograph book of animals in our backyard and called it *Animal Kingdom*, as a Christmas gift for my great-grandsons Brenner and Max.

Doug was supportive of my responsibilities and care for Gwen, who lived in Nashville, and for my mother in Bristol. For some time, I was making monthly trips to Nashville and to Bristol.

I experienced the deaths of both my step-children—Peter in 2001 and Gwen in 2009. My mother passed away in 2006. Doug helped me through these periods of grief. We also experienced the trauma from John's serious injuries from a fall and his wife Liz's ongoing complications from surgery.

In December 2015, I fell down the stairs and broke my hip and wrist. Following surgery, I spent three days in the hospital and ten days in a nursing home for rehab, coming home on December 24. Doug did a great job caring for me and doing preparations for Christmas.

In 2018, Doug decided it was time to dismantle his darkroom. After several attempts to sell or donate equipment, he came to realize it was time to junk it. We did some reorganizing of space, making the darkroom into a bedroom and another bedroom into office space for me. This took a lot of effort; the results pleased us.

Both of us made regular exercise a part of our routine. Doug rode his bike and walked through the neighborhood and on the greenways. I went to tai chi and sometimes joined Doug on his walks. We both enjoyed going to the UT Arboretum and Bissell Park for walks.

Doug and I both cared for the lawn and fishpond. Doug did all the mowing and blowing leaves off the roof. He also helped with housework and did the laundry.

Figure 16. Ebony, the cat adopted by Doug and Ruth. (2021)

In 2021, we adopted a black cat from the animal shelter and named her Ebony. It took her a few months to adjust to Doug and me and her new home. Now she is a faithful companion.

There was evidence throughout our marriage that Doug suffered from emotional problems. He had no friends, and he had cut off contact with family members.

Marriage

In October 2021, after an altercation at a restaurant, Doug spent three days at the hospital. The doctors then transferred him to Erlanger Behavioral Institute in Chattanooga where he spent ten days and was diagnosed with vascular dementia along with behavioral problems.

When Doug came home from Erlanger, he seemed to do better for a few days. Then he began refusing to take his medication, and he would not cooperate with his doctors in getting the necessary medical tests. There were signs he had had a stroke.,

On April 30, Doug collapsed and could not get up. I called our neighbor, David Glover, who helped me get Doug to the hospital emergency room. On May 5, Doug's doctors transferred him to a hospice facility in Oak Ridge, where he passed away the next day.

John came to Oak Ridge and stayed for a week to help me with many things that had to be done—taking Doug's clothes to Goodwill and guns, cameras, and other items to a pawnshop. John purchased the van that had been Doug's.

We had a memorial service at Grace Lutheran Church in July. The service was held in July because John and Liz had made plans at that time for a family vacation in the Smoky Mountains. The military honors and presenting the flag gave special meaning to the service.

My friends, Charles and Virginia Jones, had a redbud tree planted on the front lawn of Grace Lutheran Church in memory of Doug. The tree flourished and even had a few blossoms in the spring of 2023. Pastor Paula Smith dedicated the tree on June 8, 2023.

In the days and weeks following Doug's death, I experienced sorrow and loss in many ways. Doug and I had connected through a mutual interest in hiking, and now I mourned the loss of my hiking companion. I expressed my emotions by writing a poem.

Trekking Poles Who Grieve

Two sets of trekking poles stand
in the corner of the laundry room.
The tall set for Doug and the shorter
set for Ruth. The poles lean against each other
for support and comfort.
When are we going hiking? asks one
of the tall poles. *Maybe never again,*
replies the pole's mate.
*Doug is no longer with us. And Ruth
doesn't want to go without him.*

Ruth Johnson Smiley
August 2022

Reflections

I never expected to have three marriages. Instead, I dreamed of having a marriage that endured "until death do us part." My ideal family would include four children, two boys and two girls. But dreams give way to reality.

George and I were too young to be married at age 20. Ideally, two people should have completed their education and started their profession before getting married.

I have come to realize that as individuals, we become the sum of our life experiences. I believe that divorce and experiencing the deaths of two husbands have helped me become more aware, more understanding, and more compassionate of others.

And I have regrets. I regret John didn't have the stable home life with two parents that he should have had. I've read and observed that instability in relationships passes from one generation to the next, and there is evidence of that in my son's and granddaughters' lives. But we do the best we can in each situation. Hopefully, we learn from our mistakes. I have become more forgiving—forgiving of others and forgiving of myself for mistakes I have made.

I'm thankful for the understanding and support I have received from family and friends, both in the aftermath of a divorce and the deaths of two husbands. And I'm thankful for the happy times and good memories during these marriages.

My Baby Boy

Becoming a Mother

Each September, after summer heat gives way to the first signs of fall, I remember September 1958 and the birth of my son John. This brings back happy memories.

In 1958, I was 22 years old; George turned 23 just two days before John was born. We had been married two years and were living in Sutherland Village, married student housing provided by the University of Tennessee in Knoxville.

Preparing for a Baby

My pregnancy went well. I had some morning sickness early on, but it didn't last long. The odor from soup heating on a hot plate (lunch for some of my co-workers) bothered me. To this day, I don't like Campbell's soups! I was tired by the end of the day. A co-worker would give me a ride home, and I could take a nap before George got home in the evening.

My friend Peggy and her husband Charlie were living in Knoxville, waiting for his call for active duty in the Army.

My Baby Boy

Peggy's son was born in November 1957, and she loaned me all her maternity clothes. This was a great help.

In preparation for John's birth, we got an automatic washing machine. The Crumleys, Jim and Annette, gave us a bassinette, crib, and bathing table that their children had used. Grandparents, other relatives, and friends gave us many items of baby clothing. My mother, Grace Crumley, was especially generous.

George and I hoped for a baby girl. I think this was because both of us had brothers, but no sisters. The name we picked for a girl was Caroline Elizabeth. I believe this was the name of George's Grandmother Paire. We had assumed that if we had a boy, he would be George Jr.

My obstetrician was Dr. Martin Davis. At that time, women were encouraged to stay within a strict weight gain limit—mine was 20 pounds, and I managed with some effort to stay just under the limit. I never had a big appetite or tendency to gain weight before getting pregnant, but my appetite and metabolism changed completely.

After leaving my job, I had about three weeks to get work done in the apartment and prepare for a baby. One of my projects was to make a cover and skirt for the bassinette. I used pink fabric with an overlay of white organdy that had pink rosebuds sewn on—this in preparation for the girl we wanted.

I had medical insurance through the bank where I worked. George had decided that we needed more insurance, and he got a Blue Cross policy with a 10-month waiting period before it would pay maternity benefits. The doctor had said that my due date was September 19. For Blue Cross to pay, the delivery had to be no earlier than September 29—we missed it by five days!

The Big Event

George wanted to make sure we didn't make any unnecessary trips to the hospital because of false alarms. Fortunately, I didn't have any. During the afternoon of Tuesday, September 23, I began having a few twinges of early labor contractions. In the evening, Lois Hunter, our next-door neighbor, invited me over to watch TV. My contractions became stronger, and by the time I told Lois what was happening, they were five to ten minutes apart.

Lois urged me to call George and get to the hospital. We got to the University of Tennessee Hospital (where George worked in the business office) around 10 p.m. I was pretty much unprepared for what to expect. There were no classes to prepare expectant mothers and fathers for childbirth. After having the first shot of sedation, I was awake but not rational. In the delivery room, when they told me to "push," it meant no more to me than if I had been told to "fly."

My baby boy was born at 3:21 a.m., September 24, by forceps delivery. Forceps deliveries were not unusual and undoubtedly caused some injuries. (In John's case, there was later evidence that a neck injury had occurred.) He was 19 inches long and weighed 6 pounds, 14 ounces.

My Baby Boy

I did not see my baby until the nurse brought him to me in my room a few hours later. I thought he was the most beautiful baby I had ever seen, and I was not the least bit disappointed that I had a boy. Somehow, George Jr. didn't seem like the right name. We quickly decided that he would be John Maxwell Paire II, named for George's younger brother who had died in infancy.

Breast feeding was not an option because I knew I would be returning to work, and breast feeding would present complications. However, I decided I would always hold John when I fed him. I never propped his bottle, and I held him in my arms to feed him long past the time when he would have been able to hold his own bottle.

I remember the three flower arrangements I received—one from each set of grandparents and one from George.

We stayed in the hospital until Sunday (five days), much longer than is usual today. I enjoyed relaxing, feeling pampered, and having visitors. John stayed in the nursery, and the nurse brought him to me every three or four hours. On Saturday, Rob and Pauline, George's parents, came to visit us in the hospital. They brought George's Grandmother Morgan to stay for a week to help with the new baby,

On Sunday, we went home. My parents and brothers and the Crumleys from Oak Ridge came to visit. Everyone admired our new baby, and I enjoyed showing him off. However, it had been a tiring day.

After visitors had left, we prepared bottles for baby John. We mixed canned milk with a powder, put the mixture into sterilized glass bottles, and then heated the bottles for a few minutes. So, there were two daily chores with a new baby—preparing formula and washing diapers. I washed diapers inside and hung them on an outside line to dry. In bad weather, I hung them inside on a rack.

Soon after we came home from the hospital, the weather turned cooler. As a new mother, I made the mistake of putting too many layers of clothing and blankets on John, and he had a heat rash that went away soon after I removed a layer or two.

In a couple of weeks, I took John to the bank to visit my co-workers. Then we went across the street to Mayo's Garden Center, where I bought fall bulbs to plant in front of our apartment.

John had big brown eyes and what little hair he had was blonde. He was a happy baby, smiling and making little baby sounds in response to the attention he received. There were occasions when he cried to let you know he was unhappy, but they were relatively few.

We soon settled into an easy routine, with John sleeping longer intervals at night. By the time he was six weeks old, he would have a bottle around 11 p.m. and would sleep until 6 a.m.

I immediately started looking for a job and heard about a clerical position in the Dean's office at the UT College of Home Economics. Since I had been a home economics student before dropping out of college to get married, I was happy to get the job. My salary was $216 a month, just a little more than I had made at the bank. My hours were 8:30 a.m.—4:30 p.m. Monday through

Friday, and 8:30 a.m. — 12 noon on Saturday, with one Saturday a month off. I didn't like working on Saturday, but I accepted it because many jobs required Saturday work.

Then I had to make arrangements for John's care. Day care for infants was practically non-existent. Through the State Employment Office, I found an older woman, Mrs. Vess, who came to our apartment for $15 a week. I started back to work when John was six weeks old. My total maternity time between jobs was just nine weeks. Fortunately, my recovery from childbirth was without complications and John was a healthy baby.

George and I were members of nearby Bearden Methodist Church, where The Reverend Robert Parsons, formerly at Bluff City Methodist Church, was the minister. Rev. Parsons had married us, so we were happy to have him baptize John.

John's First Year

John's growth and development progressed normally, reaching milestones for turning over, sitting up, crawling, and walking a little earlier than average. He also began talking at an early age. He always seemed happy to see me when I got home from work. We bought a rocking chair, and I rocked him a lot — we both enjoyed it!

We had one near accident from using the electric space heater positioned between the bed and crib in our bedroom. I woke up during the night by the smell of something burning. A foam pillow had fallen in front of the heater, and it was melting. I picked up the pillow and quickly got it out of the house.

The secretaries in the College of Home Economics had a Christmas party in the home of one of my co-workers. I took John with me, and he was the hit of the party, sitting in his baby chair and enjoying all the attention.

We went to Bristol to visit both sets of grandparents at Christmas. On the way home, we had car trouble. I remember sitting by the stove in a car repair garage, trying to keep John warm and heat his bottle. During those days, an ongoing problem (and expense) for us was keeping the car running.

Mrs. Vess let us know in advance that she would need a week off during the spring. We asked Pauline, George's mother, if she would keep John at her home in Bristol. That was my first time away from John, and I remember how happy he looked and how happy I was to see him after a week apart.

At about that same time, Mrs. Vess gave notice that she could no longer work for us because of her health problems. It had been a great help to have Mrs. Vess come to our apartment, and I can't remember a single time that she was late or didn't show up.

Now with John about nine months old, the best childcare option was to find someone in Sutherland Village who would keep him in her apartment when I was at work. Sarah Roberts lived nearby. She had a son, Sam, who was just a little older than John, and she agreed to keep John for $10 a week.

This arrangement didn't work out satisfactorily. John cried every morning when I left him. Sarah said he cried because he missed me, and this added to my guilt feelings about leaving him. Maybe John was just going through a stage of crying, or maybe he wasn't getting enough attention from Sarah. Anyway, by the end of summer, Sarah's husband graduated, and they were moving.

Figure 17. Ruth and son John Paire (1959)

The next person I found to care for John was Wanda Cole, and she adored him. Wanda, from Middlesboro, Kentucky, was married to Earl Cole from Rose Hill, Virginia. Wanda became a second mother to John. It was a great relief to have him well cared for and happy. Wanda cared for John for nearly four years.

Becoming Independent

By the time John was a year old, he had given up his bottle but kept his pacifier. He went for regular check-ups and immunizations from the pediatrician, Dr. Stiles. John was a healthy baby, and I don't remember any illnesses during his first year.

For John's first birthday, we bought a little red wagon to give him rides around the neighborhood. Unfortunately, someone stole the wagon before John could pull it himself. Near the time of John's birthday, we moved from a one-bedroom apartment to a two-bedroom apartment in Sutherland Village.

The time of John's birth and his first year were happy times for me.

School and Work

Navigating Education and Jobs

Growing up on a farm, I learned the work ethic at an early age. My parents were hardworking, and they taught my brothers and me to follow their industrious ways.

Mama always helped with the hatchery, eggs, and bookkeeping for the farm, in addition to taking care of the house and three children. As the oldest child, Mama gave me some responsibility for looking after my two brothers and helping around the house. By the time I reached my teens, I was cooking meals on a regular basis. Also, I did weeding in the garden and lawn. Dad had an electric lawn mower with a cord, and it was my job to keep the cord out of the way as he mowed.

Occasionally, I would go to the henhouse to gather eggs. As the poultry operation increased in size, the hired man would gather eggs. Then I cleaned and packed the eggs to be sent to market. I cleaned slightly soiled eggs with a sandpaper tool. We put the dirty ones into a vinyl basket and placed it in the egg washer for a few minutes. After the eggs had drained and dried, I packed them in crates—always the small end of the egg was packed down. We kept cracked eggs separate. A few people came by regularly to buy cracked eggs for a nominal sum. This was probably a holdover from the Great Depression.

One of my chores was to keep the stoker that fed the furnace filled with coal. Dad brought coal (like small pebbles) to a chute that went into the basement, and I shoveled coal into the stoker once a day. The job took just a few minutes. One day I forgot to do this chore. When the house got cold that night, Dad woke me to go to the basement and do my job. After that, I remembered!

My parents never gave me an allowance or pay for doing chores. If I wanted money to buy something, I had to ask. Although Mama was usually generous, I wanted to have money of my own.

My introduction to learning was through Sunday School and Vacation Bible Schools at Silver Grove Lutheran Church and Weavers Union Church during the summer. I remember how we lined up on the outside steps at Weavers and that musty smell as we marched into the basement singing "Onward Christian Soldiers."

Weavers Elementary School (1942-1950)

Weavers Elementary School, Weavers Union Church, and Rader's Store formed the center of the Weavers community on Weaver Pike. This was about two miles from our home on Paddle Creek Road. Over the years, I walked to the store when Mama needed bread or some other item. There was always money for me to have a treat from the store—usually a Grape or Orange

Becoming Independent

Crush soda from the big cooler in the store and a small bag of potato chips.

When I was walking, there were occasions when someone stopped to give me a ride. These people probably knew who I was, but I didn't always know them. Nevertheless, I accepted a ride. No one ever warned me not to accept rides from strangers.

There was no kindergarten in the school system. Weavers Elementary School had eight grades, with a total around 200 students. By the time I started first grade, I was six and a half years old. In advance of the first day of school, Mama took me to register and get the required vaccinations. On the first day of school, I went alone on the school bus. When I got on the bus to go home in the afternoon, I asked the bus driver if this was the Paddle Creek Road bus. He assured me I was getting on the right bus. It impressed the driver that I was looking out for myself, and he told my mother about the incident. My parents were also impressed. Perhaps this indicated my independent nature and the fact that I could take care of myself.

I liked school from the very beginning. My first-grade teacher was Miss Pauline Groseclose. I became very fond of her. Soon I was learning reading, writing (cursive, of course), and arithmetic. At mid-year, I moved to a second level, and Miss Ada Lynn Feathers was my teacher. I liked her, but I still missed Miss Groseclose. The two adjacent classrooms were in the basement, with the boys' restroom at one end and the girls' restroom at the other end. To get from my classroom to the girls' restroom, you had to walk through Miss Groseclose's classroom. I missed her

School and Work

so much that I was making frequent trips to the restroom until Miss Feathers caught on to what was going on.

A few of the students I started with in first grade continued with me through high school—Edna Burnett, JoAnn Galliher, David Reece, Eugene Booher, and perhaps one or two more.

It was a few years before the school served lunches, so I took a packed lunch. When the school lunch program began, lunches were 10 cents. I didn't care much for the lunches—I especially disliked the times when we had pinto beans, cornbread, and greens.

World War II came about in my early school years. I remember our teachers asked us to collect milkweed pods to be used for making parachutes. Because of gasoline rationing, the bus made fewer stops, and this meant I had to walk a short distance to the bus stop. I heard German submarines were coming near the east coast—this made me glad we were living inland!

Teachers encouraged students to buy war bonds. There were stamp books, and I believe each stamp cost a quarter. When we filled a book, we exchanged it for a $25 bond. I had a few bonds I saved and cashed when I entered college. At Mama's urging, I wrote letters to Uncle Clyde who was in the Navy serving on a ship in the Pacific.

Each year, the school had an operetta. In the fourth grade, I had the part of a fairy (I don't remember the name of the operetta). On the day of the performance, I wasn't feeling well and didn't go to school. I took part in the performance that night, however. The next day, it was obvious I had measles. Along with the red rash on my skin, I had a fever. It took me about a week to recover.

The school principal when I began school was Miss Thelma Rotenberry. Mr. Paul Stone, who was also my eighth-grade teacher, succeeded Miss Rotenberry as principal. My other teachers (all unmarried women) were Miss Groseclose, third grade; Miss Louise Morton, fourth grade; Miss Ruby O'Dell, fifth grade; Miss Evelyn O'Dell, sixth grade; and Miss Louise Brown, seventh grade. I can remember each teacher and each grade except for the sixth grade. I'm not aware of what might have happened during the sixth grade that made me forget that year. At a high school class reunion, I asked David Reese who our sixth-grade teacher had been, and he told me it was Miss Evelyn O'Dell (a sister of Miss Ruby O'Dell).

I liked all my teachers and enjoyed each grade except for the seventh. Miss Brown was a nervous person who didn't enjoy teaching. Her method of teaching was to write questions on the board. We were to read our books and write answers to her questions. She did a lot of chewing on her pencils and yelling at students.

I was always a good student. My parents didn't stress the importance of doing well in school—it was just expected that I would make good grades.

I enjoyed reading. Books that I remember reading were the Bobbsey Twins and Nancy Drew series, *Heidi*, *Sleeping Beauty*, and *Little Women*. When I was in about the fifth or sixth grade,

School and Work

Mama bought a set of Compton's Encyclopedias, which expanded my access to learning. Now I had information at hand when I had to write a paper on an assigned topic.

Religion was part of the school program. Each day began with scripture reading and prayer. Sometimes students quoted a Bible verse. The most often quoted was "Jesus wept." The Reverend Paul Doring made regular visits to the school and spoke to students in the school auditorium. Rev. Doring gave rewards for memorizing Bible verses, and I received a Bible in 1948. I gave this Bible to my great-grandson Brenner a few years ago.

The Women's Christian Temperance Union visited our school and asked students to sign pledge cards saying we wouldn't drink alcohol, smoke, or use profanity. I remember some of the words ". . . from all tobacco I'll abstain and never take God's name in vain." I've kept the pledge on these items, but not the one about alcohol.

Other friends in elementary school included Betty Lou Freeman, Joanne O'Dell, Ann Wicker, Margie Brown, Mitzi Widner, Connie Widner, Don Cole, Charles Gray, and Francis Greene. I occasionally visited girlfriends in their homes and would stay overnight. However, I did not feel free to have them come to my home—for whatever reason, my parents didn't encourage me to invite friends.

I have not kept in touch with these friends from elementary school, although I have seen some of them at high school reunions. Edna Burnett reminded me we knew each other at Bible

School even before we started first grade together. Many of these friends from elementary school are now deceased.

In most respects, I feel I got a good basic education in my elementary years. I remember Mr. Stone taught us the rules of grammar, punctuation, and diagramming sentences. The reading and writing skills I learned gave me a foundation for high school, college, and the jobs I've had.

At about the time I entered high school, Dad was taking one-day courses on poultry offered at the University of Tennessee's College of Agriculture, and he would take me along. He had his Cessna plane, and we flew into the Island Home Airport in Knoxville. He did not have a radio and there was no air traffic control at this airport. I remember the time we were coming in for a landing, and I saw another plane that looked like it was getting ready to land. I asked Dad if he had seen it. He said "no," and he was glad I saw the plane and alerted him about it.

I sat through the classes. I can't say that I learned anything, but it was my first introduction to college. This may have had something to do with my ambition to attend UT.

Bluff City High School (1950-1954)

I got on the bus for high school each morning along with Don and Claude. Claude was now in the fifth grade, and Don was entering first grade. The bus was overcrowded with standing room only—unsafe by today's standards. The bus dropped off

School and Work

students at Weavers Elementary and continued to Bluff City about ten miles away.

There were about 300 students in the high school. The principal when I began was Mr. J. H. Pierce, followed by Mr. Kenneth Carrier. As I recall, students liked both principals, and the school had few discipline problems.

My freshman classes included algebra, English, general science, and home economics. I liked the classes and my teachers. Miss Alice Hicks, my English teacher, and Mrs. Sibyl Milhorn, my algebra teacher, had my dad as a student when he was at Bluff City High School.

Ruth Blevins was in the freshman class—the only Ruth I remember from either elementary or high school. My home economics teacher was always getting the two of us mixed up, and I think I got a lower grade as a result. I got a grade of 90 for the first six weeks reporting period, and this was lower than my grades in other classes.

Teachers gave numerical grades. I had an average of 96.875 for the year in all classes (I still have my report cards). This gave me the distinction of "Honor Student" for having the highest grade average of the entire student body of around 300 students. This surprised and pleased me!

I had started piano lessons in the fourth grade but did not continue because the teacher quit coming to our school. I resumed piano lessons when I started high school, but my heart was not in it. My teacher rapped my fingers with a pencil when I made a mistake. Besides that, I lacked musical talent and a burning desire to learn. After I got the Honor Student award, my teacher said something to the effect that "You must not have had time for the piano." I gave it up. I had learned to play "Silent Night" and "I'm Dreaming of a White Christmas."

In the summer of 1952, Weavers Community Club, an organization of citizens in the area, sponsored me as a candidate for Independence Day queen in the annual county-wide festival held in Blountville. The club gave me a bouquet of roses, and I had a new evening dress. A panel of three judges selected the queen in what might be called a beauty contest. I couldn't believe that I won! My parents thought my stage presence—that is, the way I walked slowly and confidently across the stage—made the judges choose me. Perhaps the judges took notice of me because I was the last of the 12 candidates to walk across the stage.

Illness disrupted my sophomore year in high school. During an outbreak of infectious hepatitis in the elementary school, Claude, Dad, and I all came down with it around Thanksgiving. I remember not being able to keep food or drink, including water down, and we developed that yellow color. In fact, some people referred to the illness as yellow jaundice.

Mama called a doctor who came to our house. I don't remember what treatment, if any, he prescribed. When we were not getting any better, Mama called a second doctor who asked Dad what medication he was taking. Don ran to get it and came back with a bottle of whiskey, much to everyone's chagrin. A visiting neighbor had brought this to dad to make him feel better. My parents were strict teetotalers, but Dad's denial that he was drinking the whiskey did not convince the doctor. He went on to lecture Dad about the damage alcohol would do to his liver during this illness.

I missed school the entire time between Thanksgiving and Christmas—17 days. And in the spring, I got mumps and missed nine days of school. My grades suffered somewhat because of my absences, but I still managed to maintain a high average.

Shortly before I came down with mumps, there was a 4-H Club party, and I had my first date at age 16. I remember standing in the school hallway near my locker when I asked Francis Greene if he would come to the party with me. He hesitated slightly and told me he didn't have a driver's license. I suggested we might go with another couple. As it turned out, we went with Joanne O'Dell and Ross Perry. I was certainly ahead of the times in asking a boy for a date!

Basketball games were the highlight of extracurricular activities. There was no football team or band. I attended only four or five games during the time I was in high school, and this was a continuing conflict between my parents and me. Transportation was the major issue. I could have taken a school bus that ran right by our house to the games, but my parents perceived that a lot of necking (as we called it then) took place in the dark on the ride home. Somehow, and I don't know how I managed it, I remember taking the bus to a game just once. There were a few occasions that I went with Uncle Haskel or cousins June and Velma McClelland. It was not that I had an interest in basketball, but I wanted to be part of school activities.

Becoming Independent

The community had strict social mores about what social activities they permitted. Dancing was taboo, although they accepted square dancing if we called it "folk dancing." Some churches had social activities for high school students, but my church was too small to have a youth group.

I vaguely remember a party at someone's home where we played spin the bottle. For those who don't know this game, girls would sit in a circle and boys would take turns going to the center and spinning the bottle. Then the boy got to kiss whichever girl the bottle pointed to when it stopped spinning.

The worst possible fate for an unmarried girl was to get pregnant. I did not know of any instances of pregnancy among the high school girls. If this happened, the family kept it well hidden. There was no such thing as sex education in high school. In health classes (separate for boys and girls), the teacher presented basic facts about menstruation and pregnancy. I remember the teacher saying that she would not discuss contraception, implying that we didn't need to know, lest this would lead to sexual activity.

In my junior and senior years, I began typing classes, taught by Mrs. Bonnie Prince. The skills I learned there have served me well ever since. I learned to type on a manual typewriter, and it was not until years later that I used an IBM electric typewriter. The home economics classes had both pedal and electric sewing machines. The kitchen contained an electric range, but no microwave oven or dishwasher.

School and Work

Figure 18. Ruth (right) with classmates at Bluff City High School commencement. Senator Estes Kefauver spoke. (1953)

In my junior year, Senator Estes Kefauver spoke at the high school commencement, and I had the privilege of being among those pictured with him. I first remember hearing about Senator Kefauver when he sought the Democratic nomination for president in 1952. While I worked in the egg room packing eggs as one of my chores on the farm, I listened to the Democratic National Convention on the radio. This was my first interest in politics. Although Kefauver had received the most votes in the state primaries, he lost the nomination to Adlai Stevenson at the convention.

In my junior year, a new student, George Paire, came to BCHS. George attracted attention because of his dark hair combed into a ducktail, and his clothes that contrasted with the country-boy jeans worn by most of the male students.

Living in a community where my ancestors had settled around 1789, there were numerous familial connections among people, as I think back now. Mrs. Ruth Boy Stone, the school librarian, was a cousin of Dad's, and my parents named me for her. Two teachers were relatives through the Thomas family (my mother's family): Mrs. Mona Thomas Rutherford and Mrs. Helen Thomas. Mr. Carrier, the school principal, was married to a member of the Boy family (my father's side). Virginia Hancher was related through my father's side of the family. Two first cousins, June and Velma McClelland also attended BCHS during my time there. I didn't realize at the time that another student, Toni Spears, was a distant cousin through the Thomas family. There were likely other relatives that I wasn't aware of. I didn't give much thought about family connections. It was years later, after I became involved in genealogy, that I realized I had all these relatives.

I had a part in the junior class play, "Mammy's Li'l Wild Rose." I don't remember my character, but I wasn't one of those who had to black their faces to appear as Black people. Students and the community accepted this practice without question.

George had a part in the senior class play, "Seventeenth Summer." In the yearbook picture of this play, George is wearing a black shirt with a white tie. I recall someone remarking that "George liked to be different—if everyone else was wearing a white shirt with a black tie, he did the opposite."

School and Work

Later, I realized the deficiencies in my high school education. I remember little from a class in American history. Either I didn't find it of interest or the teacher didn't make it interesting. Since I had plans to study home economics in college, teachers advised me I didn't need to take math classes beyond the first year of algebra. After I got to college, I realized the importance of math in many areas and I took a remedial class.

Teachers advised me to take chemistry; however, the class was a disaster. The man who taught the class, newly retired from Tennessee Eastman Company, knew little about teaching. He gave up on teaching and let us do whatever we wanted in class and labs. He let us use our textbook during tests. Needless to say, I suffered from this experience when I took chemistry in college.

Two automobile accidents cast a pall over BCHS during my senior year. Rhonda Perry, Ray Messimer, Billy Malone, Dean Ray, and Philip Malone lost their lives in a car accident on October 10, 1953. Evidence showed the car had been traveling at a high speed, probably racing against another car. Rhonda, Ray, and Billy were members of the senior class. Joe Lee Harrington, who was a neighbor of my family, died in an accident on February 4, 1954.

In our senior year, class members voted David Reece and me "most likely to succeed." David earned a degree in electrical engineering from the University of Tennessee and went to work for a utility company in Massachusetts. On a trip to the northeast in 1981, I visited David and his wife Joan in their home. It was evident that David had succeeded—good job, beautiful home, and stable marriage.

There were 63 students in my graduating class. I was class valedictorian, and Betty Lou Freeman, my classmate since elementary school, was salutatorian. I received a letter of congratulations from Governor Frank Clement. The caption by my picture in the yearbook says, "The first path to success is wanting it."

The few career opportunities considered suitable for women were teaching, nursing, and secretarial positions. My role models were the 4-H Extension Agents in Sullivan County—Miss Rowena Keck and Mrs. Elsie Lee Smalling. I wanted to study home economics in college and become an Extension Agent. Through the 4-H Club, I had received a scholarship to attend Virginia Intermont College, a two-year college for women in Bristol. My parents wanted me to go there and take business courses so that I could help with management of the farm. However, I had my heart set on attending the University of Tennessee. I applied for a scholarship and received a $300 scholarship from the Sears-Roebuck Foundation. That amount of money went a long way in those days; tuition for a year (three quarters) was $159! With the scholarship, my parents consented for me to go to UT. Getting me away from George probably had something to do with it. He planned to attend East Tennessee State College (now University).

School and Work

The University of Tennessee (1954-1955)

Entering college was both challenging and a big adjustment. I lived in Henson Hall, the freshman girls' dormitory. For me, it meant more freedom than I had at home. The curfew was 9:30 on weeknights, 12:00 on Friday and Saturday, and 10:45 on Sunday. When we went out for the evening, we had to sign out and sign in when we returned. We wore skirts to classes. If we were wearing shorts to go to the gym, we had to wear a raincoat over the shorts. Boys could visit girls in the first-floor lounge—not in the girls' room. We had a housemother, Bertie, who enforced the rules.

Each floor had a large, shared bathroom. And there was one telephone in the hallway on each floor. It was up to the person who answered the phone to find whoever was wanted on the phone and to take messages—not a very efficient system.

My roommate was Mary Kay Bachman, who had been one of my classmates at BCHS. We were congenial, but each had our own interests and a different set of friends. Kay was an art major and in a sorority. I never considered joining a sorority because of the cost, plus my parents would not approve of what they saw as just a social organization.

With the first gathering of girls for a meeting in the dorm lounge, I saw the majority smoked. I never took up smoking because my one attempt seemed very unpleasant to me. I didn't want to spend the money, and I knew my parents would strongly disapprove.

Becoming Independent

It was difficult for me to get enough sleep because the dorm didn't quieten down until around midnight. Our room on the third floor was directly above the front entrance, so we heard everyone coming and going. I found it easier to do most of my studying in the library between classes, and sometimes I would get back to the dorm for a daytime nap.

Gail Smith and Amy Wing lived across the hall from my room, and we became friends. Amy and her family lived in Memphis, having come from Canton, China in the late 1940s. Amy had a habit of getting up in the morning, still blinking her eyes and opening the door to our room. She wouldn't say anything; it was like she was checking to see who was there. Amy and I remained in contact until her death a few years ago.

Gail Smith, from Lenoir City, married Richard Marius in the summer of 1955, and I was in their wedding. Richard became a well-known college professor. Their marriage didn't last.

Peggy Staniforth, from Erwin, became my best friend, and we stayed in touch through the years. Other close friends were Norma Tate from Chattanooga and Lois Breazeale from Lenoir City. All three friends are now deceased.

I got a job working 10 to 15 hours per week in the cafeteria at Strong Hall, located just across Cumberland Avenue from Henson Hall. I served food to students as they came through the line. The pay was one meal for each hour worked. If you had unused hours at the end of the month, you were paid 40 cents per hour.

School and Work

Few students had cars. It was easy to get around Knoxville by bus, and the fare was affordable for students. I took the Greyhound bus from Knoxville to Bristol when I went home for the weekend. Occasionally, I took the train to Johnson City, along with Peggy, whose father worked for the railroad. My uncle and aunt, Jim and Annette Crumley, lived in Oak Ridge, and I would visit them from time to time, taking my laundry with me.

Registering for classes each quarter was a nightmare! Nothing was automated, of course. Each student met with a faculty advisor who approved a course load, and each student registered at their appointment time. Registration took place in a large gym. Departments had registration tables, and you had to stand in line to get your name on the registration list for the class you wanted. To get there before classes filled, you hoped to be lucky enough to get an early appointment time. The registration process took hours!

One year of chemistry was required for all home economics students. In my class, there were very few girls in a lecture of 100 or more students. We had lab once a week, with a graduate student as instructor for a group of about 12 students. One instructor was especially helpful and spent extra time with two or three of us who were having trouble. My difficulty came from poor preparation in high school. I struggled to make a C. Despite this, my grade point average was above 3.0 for my freshman year.

I enjoyed English classes and especially liked Miss Pennebaker, who was my instructor for two quarters. One story she told about her life in the East Tennessee Bible Belt remains in my memory. A proselytizing evangelist came to her door. This person told Miss Pennebaker that "her soul was damned to hell just like the soul of her dog" who was watching this encounter. Miss Pennebaker replied, "Say whatever you want about me, but you can't say that about my dog!" Miss Pennebaker later married a UT professor. Sadly, he died in a plane crash, along with several other local people, in route from Washington to Knoxville.

I also remember a psychology professor who liked to poke fun at "the man who sells beans," referring to Cas Walker, a controversial politician. Cas, as most people called him, served as mayor of Knoxville and he owned several grocery stores.

The only grade of D I received in college was in modern dance, a physical education class. My preference was to take tap dancing, but all the classes were filled when I registered. Miss Dorothy Floyd taught the class. For the final exam, each student was to give a solo performance of a dance, choosing her own music and choreography. I purchased a record of "Ebb Tide" and tried to come up with movements I could do. But on the scheduled day to give my solo, I just couldn't bring myself to do it. Later, I told Miss Floyd that I didn't have a good excuse for not showing up. I was fortunate that she gave me a D instead of an F!

I had a student pass for football games (very cheap), and I attended a few home games, although I never became a football fan. The star player was Johnny Majors, who was named SEC player of the year by the *Nashville Banner* in 1955 and again in

School and Work

1956. After playing football, he went into coaching and eventually returned to UT as coach.

Nearby restaurants included the Tea Room, G & H (students called it "Gag & Heave") and the Tennessean. Dixieland was on Kingston Pike. Popular nightspots included the Doggy Patch and Highlands Grill. I didn't venture far from campus, but I remember when my roommate's mother visited and took us to Dixieland.

Panty raids were a college campus craze throughout the country during the 1950s, and UT was no exception. The raids at Henson Hall occurred two or three times during my freshman year. After the dorm closed for the night, a large group of male students gathered outside, shouting and threatening to come inside (they never did). And they didn't have to! Girls came to the windows to see what was going on. Some girls entered the game by shouting and throwing panties to the boys. Believe me, I had no part in this!

Peggy and I became roommates at the beginning of our sophomore year. Our room was at the end of the hallway and much quieter than the one I was in my freshman year. The quiet room was a good arrangement for both Peggy and me.

George and I continued our romance. I saw him whenever I went back home for a visit, and he came to Knoxville to see me a few times. We began discussing marriage, and our plan was that both of us would work part-time, and we would continue our education. George wanted to go to law school after completing a bachelor's degree.

During Thanksgiving vacation of 1955, we brought up these plans with my parents. I remember a brief discussion when we were standing in the kitchen; they didn't suggest that we sit down together and discuss this. The next week, I got a phone call from Mama asking that I come home that weekend. This was not a good time for me to leave campus because final exams were beginning. Anyway, I went home.

The result was that my parents said that they wouldn't pay for me to go to school the remainder of my sophomore year if I intended to get married. However, I took final exams and completed the fall quarter.

I would have liked to stay in Knoxville and found a job, but my parents strongly objected, and I didn't have money to get started. My parents offered me $100 a month to work on the farm, but I looked for a job in Bristol instead, and I lived at home. George went to Flint, Michigan, where he planned to find a job in the auto industry. Our plan was that after we both worked for a while and saved some money, we would get married.

Inter-Mountain Telephone Company (1956)

I went to the State Employment Office in Bristol and was referred to Inter-Mountain Telephone Company. They immediately offered me a job at $145 a month (minimum wage). I worked on long-distance telephone billing with several other women in an office, one of whom was Mary Jo Harbour, who had

School and Work

been one of my high school classmates. Our supervisor was Miss Della Sweeney.

The first task was to sort small slips of paper that the operator filled out for each long-distance call. We had to sort these slips of paper by billing number, and this took several steps. Then, when we had separated papers for each billing number, we added the charges for a monthly bill on a type of adding machine called a Comptometer. The final step was to verify the telephone number for each bill. It was a slow process, like many other jobs before we had computers.

During the time I worked there, they increased the minimum wage and raised my pay to $175 a month. I rode with a neighbor, Mr. Simcox, to Bristol each day, and I paid him $3.00 a week. Another neighbor, Mrs. Ruth Morrell, rode with us.

I borrowed money from my brother Don to begin UT correspondence courses in economics and English literature. I never completed the courses, for two reasons. One was that after working all day and coming home to cook supper, I didn't have much energy for studies. Another reason was that I got C grades on the first assignments I submitted. That was discouraging.

I went to visit my friends at UT on my birthday weekend in February. Norma and her boyfriend, Bill Robertson (later married) picked me up from the bus station, and we grabbed hamburgers at Babe Malloy's on Chapman Highway. Conveniently, Peggy's new roommate was away, and I stayed in our old room. My friends had a birthday cake for me—this was the first birthday cake I ever had!

BECOMING INDEPENDENT

Tennessee Valley Bank (1956-1958)

Bearden Branch of the Tennessee Valley Bank was on Kingston Pike next to the post office. It was across the street from Long's Drug Store and Mayo Garden Center. There were no banks further west on Kingston Pike.

Bank management hired me because of the branch manager's illness; they thought he needed some help. Mr. Martin Coykendall was branch manager; Mr. James Chambers was assistant manager. Tellers were Mrs. Sue Moore, Mrs. Jean Redmond, and Mrs. Mary Lynn Moses. A part-time student worker came in after bank closing to compile and tally checks that were transmitted to the main office. A Black janitor, Mack, came late in the day to clean.

George took me to work in the morning, and I rode the bus home in the afternoon. On Fridays, I would usually walk to the nearby White Store to do my weekly grocery shopping, and George would meet me there.

I was the teller who took care of several tasks—opening new accounts, ordering checks, and sales of travelers' checks, cashier's checks, and savings bonds. I also took deposits and cashed checks when there were long lines at the other tellers' windows.

The bank opened at 8:00 a.m. and closed at 2:00 p.m. On Fridays, we reopened from 4:00 p.m to 6:00 p.m. After closing, each teller had to balance her records, all done with only an adding machine. Tellers reconciled most discrepancies, but not

School and Work

all. A teller did not have to make up a shortage, but errors became part of a teller's job performance record.

On a Friday afternoon in the fall of 1956, I began experiencing dizziness and feeling ill while at work. I went home and got into bed. The next morning, I didn't feel any better, and my left ear seemed to be stopped up. I visited a doctor, who couldn't find anything to explain what was happening to me. The dizziness and other symptoms cleared up, but I had lost most of the hearing in my left ear.

Later tests at the UT Hearing and Speech Center showed that I had suffered damage to the auditory nerves; thus, a hearing aid would not help. I adjusted to the hearing loss. However, I can't hear sounds coming from the left or tell the direction a sound is coming from.

Banking was much less competitive in the 1950s. According to popular belief, bankers operated under the 3-6-3 rule—they paid three percent interest on deposits, made loans at six percent interest, and got to the golf course by 3:00. There were four banks in Knoxville: Hamilton National Bank, Park National Bank, Bank of Knoxville, and Tennessee Valley Bank. Bank policies helped keep wages low. Employees were not supposed to discuss how much they made, and a bank would not accept a job application from someone already employed at another bank.

My beginning salary was $175 a month. After one year, I got a $10 raise to $185 a month. On the anniversary of my second year, I did not get a raise because I was pregnant and would be leaving my job. There was no such thing as maternity leave. A woman was supposed to leave by the time she was "showing." As it turned out, I worked until three weeks before my due date. I had trained someone to replace me, but she had to resign because of medical problems. Then I trained a second person, and I left my job just before Labor Day.

The University of Tennessee (1958-1962)

My friend Lois told me about a job opening in the Dean's office at the UT College of Home Economics. Since I had been a home economics major before dropping out of college to get married, I was happy to get the job. My salary was $216 a month, just a little more than I had made at the bank. My hours were 8:30 a.m.—4:30 p.m. Monday through Friday and 8:30 a.m.—12 noon on Saturday, with one Saturday a month off. I didn't like working on Saturday but accepted it because many jobs required Saturday work.

Miss Ida Anders was acting dean, followed by Dr. Lura Odland, who became dean about a year later. The four office employees included Miss Mildred Ayers, who maintained student records; Mrs. Ruth Brown, the dean's secretary; Mrs. Nancy Colquitt, bookkeeper; and my position as a "general flunky."

The first year when Miss Anders was dean, the office staff was not very busy. Most of what I did was type on a manual typewriter with carbon copies and using an eraser to make corrections. I typed stencils to make mimeograph copies. I also used the mimeograph machine, and I remember it as a messy job!

Dean Odland set about making changes soon after she arrived. She moved Mrs. Brown to another office, and made me the dean's secretary, but I did not immediately receive a salary increase to go with the added responsibilities. Later, I had a job offer from Oak Ridge National Laboratory. Dean Odland then offered me a raise to stay, and I did, although the salary was not as high as what I could have made at ORNL.

Dean Odland used a Dictaphone to record her letters and other items. I listened to the recordings and typed drafts and edited them before I did the final copies. Dean Odland complimented me on how I could take what she gave me and put it in good form—"make her look good," as she put it.

When Dean Odland learned I was interested in completing my degree, she gave me permission to take one class a quarter during work hours. I did not have to make up the time. This was a real boost in my goal to get a degree.

George finished his law degree and passed the bar exam in 1962. He got a job with State Farm as an insurance adjuster, as many law graduates did, to get experience and earn some money. He had to be out of town for one month's training, so this meant I had to learn to drive. I got an instructor from a driving school and got my driver's license within a few weeks, learning to drive a Volkswagen Beetle with a stick shift. Now it was my turn to finish my degree. I resigned from my job to become a full-time student.

BECOMING INDEPENDENT

After six months, George left State Farm to go into law practice. This meant I had to give up my education and find a job to support us while he became established in law practice.

Oak Ridge Institute of Nuclear Studies (1963-1969)

After making a few contacts and filling out job applications, Oak Ridge Institute of Nuclear Studies offered me a job in the administrative office of the Medical Division, a cancer research and hospital facility. My job title was record clerk, and I worked for Mr. J. Howard Harmon, the administrative officer.

My duties included collecting weekly timecards from all employees and checking them for obvious errors and inconsistencies. I received bi-weekly paychecks, and each employee stopped by my office to pick up their check. Thus, I became acquainted with the more than one hundred employees in the Medical Division.

I handled purchasing requests. I typed the requisitions and got the necessary approvals before sending them to the purchasing department.

Mr. Harmon oversaw the division budget and troubleshooting whatever problems came up. There was never a dull moment!

Dr. Gould Andrews, division chairman, and Dr. Ralph Kniseley, assistant chairman, were compassionate doctors who cared about their patients and appreciated the work of the division employees. I have a personal letter from Dr. Andrews

School and Work

who thanked me for my part in arranging a successful medical symposium. Mrs. Betty Anderson, technical editor, was especially helpful to the clerical staff. She made us feel that our work was important. Office employees included Mrs. Willa Fae Loveday, Mrs. Jane Fuqua, Mrs. Sandra Williams, and Mrs. Mona Isbell Smith. Mona and I reconnected recently, and she is now my Facebook friend.

I will never forget one big goof I made. Willa Fae, who handled travel arrangements, gave me instructions for what I was to do during her absence. I picked up the plane tickets and scheduled the limousine according to the itinerary Willa Fae had given me. The problem was that I didn't check flight time on the plane ticket—it had changed from what was on the itinerary. Dr. Gengozian got to the airport about three hours before the flight time. He was furious, and I was mortified!

The Medical Division had a grant from NASA to collect and analyze data on the effects of radiation exposure just as the computer era was beginning. We got a couple of keypunch machines to enter data on punched cards. I learned to do this, and it turned out to be a skill that I used later. The division hired Miss Marian Oates for the NASA project, and we became lifelong friends until her death from breast cancer a few years ago.

Following my divorce from George, I didn't see any future in my job, so I went back to school. I cashed in the retirement funds I had accumulated (about $2,000) and got a small scholarship and a student loan. My parents generously contributed $1,000, and

George voluntarily increased his monthly child support payment from $100 to $150. I was on my way!

The University of Tennessee (1969-1971)

I was 33 years old and back on the college campus as a student! Not much had changed in the six years since I had worked there. Many of the faculty members I had known were still at UT, and they gave me a warm welcome back. I drove to campus each day from our home in Concord.

I continued to work toward my degree in home economics. However, after taking the required courses in economics (taught in the College of Business Administration), I found my interests evolving toward this field. I majored in family and consumer economics within the College of Home Economics curriculum. I hoped to fulfill my long-time goal of becoming an extension agent after I earned my degree. Sometimes I worried that the fact I was divorced might adversely affect my chances of getting a job offer.

One of my economics instructors, a PhD candidate at UT, had taught at King College in Bristol, and I learned that my brother Claude had been one of his students. He told me that "Claude was one of the best students he ever had." He then said, "No, Claude was *the best* student I ever had."

I took a class in Fortran but never had the occasion to use it. However, it proved to be a useful introduction to computers and logical thinking. This was the era of punched cards. For homework assignments, I had to punch my cards and turn them in at the computing center. Then I picked up results the next day. It was costly to make an error—another day to complete the assignment!

Through my academic standing, Phi Kappa Phi, a scholastic honorary society, and Omicron Nu, the home economics honorary society, invited me to join. I represented the UT chapter of Omicron Nu, with expenses paid, at the national meeting of Omicron Nu at Colorado State University in Fort Collins. John stayed with my parents during the week I was away.

As I was nearing the completion of my bachelor's degree, several faculty members encouraged me to go on for a master's degree. I applied for a couple of fellowships and got both! However, the rules kept me from accepting more than one.

I got my bachelor's degree in June 1970—it took me 16 years! As the graduate with the highest GPA in the College of Home Economics, I led the procession of home economics graduates into the gym at commencement. John, my parents, and Bill Johnson were there to see me graduate.

Miss Phyllis Ilett was my major professor for the graduate program, with a major in family economics and a minor in economics. Dr. Keith E. Phillips, economics professor, and Dr. Peggy S. Berger, family economics professor, were members of my graduate committee along with Professor Ilett.

For my master's thesis, I interviewed 50 families in Knoxville, Tennessee, who had purchased homes as part of a government program that lowered mortgage interest rates. The title of my thesis was "Home Ownership Attitudes and Housing Satisfactions of Families Who Have Received Assistance Under Section 235 of the Housing and Urban Development Act of 1968." I had a professional service to format and type my thesis. I felt it was well worth the cost.

My thesis acknowledgements include the following statement: "Special thanks are given to John Paire for his patience, cooperation, and interest in his mother's graduate studies, and to Mr. R. William Johnson for his role as critic and proofreader."

In June 1971, I received my master's degree, married Bill Johnson, and moved to Oak Ridge.

I soon discovered that finding a job in Oak Ridge suited to my area of study would not be easy. Teaching was not an option because I had not met the requirements for teacher certification. And there were very few openings for extension agents in Tennessee and none in the county where I lived. An agent was required to live in the county where he or she worked.

UT Agricultural Extension Service employed me on a short-term contract to conduct household interviews in Morgan and Hawkins Counties. The interviews were part of a study to aid the extension service in program planning to meet the needs of rural Tennesseans.

For several weeks, I made the long drive from home in Oak Ridge to Morgan County. Then I stayed with my parents in Bristol and drove to nearby Hawkins County to do the interviews there.

School and Work

Overall, I enjoyed the experience. People were cooperative and willing to talk. I can remember just two people who declined to do an interview. I never felt unsafe or threatened, unlike what I might feel in a similar situation today.

Anderson County Day Care (1972-1973)

I learned about the federally funded day care program through a newspaper story. I contacted Mr. James Zitzman of Oak Ridge Schools and he employed me as a social worker for the program in Oak Ridge. It was my job to enroll children, determine income eligibility, and serve as a liaison between the day care center and the child's home. Through this work, I became acquainted with some of the lower-income sections of Oak Ridge, including the Black community of Scarboro.

It was hard for me not to take problems home with me. I soon came to realize that I was more concerned about my clients' problems than some of them seemed to be. There was also the uncertainty about how long program funding would last. For these reasons, I was happy to find another job.

City of Oak Ridge (1973-1979)

Reading the *Oak Ridger* newspaper proved to be a good way to find job leads. I read that the City of Oak Ridge was beginning a home management service funded by the electric department. I learned that the city manager, Mr. Carleton McMullin, became interested in initiating this program through his daughter who was a home economics student at UT. Perhaps she gave him the idea.

The City of Oak Ridge hired me at an annual salary of $8,500; my job title was home management aide. Shortly thereafter, Mr. McMullin left Oak Ridge for another job. Mr. William Haddock succeeded him, first as acting city manager and then as city manager. The administration gave me a desk in the crowded and noisy finance department, in the municipal building, with little in the way of support or funds for the program.

Miss Winnie Bowman, Tennessee Valley Authority (TVA) home economist, helped me get started. TVA initiated a home economics program in the early days to promote the use of electric appliances. By the 1970s, the emphasis was on conserving energy.

To get information to the public, we planned an evening program with refreshments in the auditorium of the Oak Ridge Public Library. I mailed invitation letters to education, civic, and social organizations in the city and got an article in the *Oak Ridger*. I had no idea how many to expect—maybe 50. As it turned out, only five or six showed up! It was a big disappointment, but a beginning. Gradually, groups were inviting me to present a program, and individuals were calling me with questions. I communicated information to the public through radio programs, newsletters, news articles, seminars, and workshops. I worked with the Oak Ridge School System, Agricultural

Extension Service, Community Action Commission, YWCA, and other groups.

When I learned of an upcoming office vacancy at the city's municipal building, I immediately asked for the office, and I got my own small office next to the health department. The city assigned me to the health department, with Mr. Joe Mitchell as my supervisor.

After about five years on this job, I began thinking about returning to UT to get a PhD. I've said that whenever I got bored with a job, I went back to school! I wanted to further my interest in economics, and I applied to the Department of Agricultural Economics in the UT College of Agriculture. But first, I made sure that there was no longer a foreign language requirement in the PhD program. I thought it was too late in life for me to learn a foreign language.

The University of Tennessee and Oak Ridge National Laboratory (1979-1981)

Not only was I accepted in the PhD program, UT gave me a graduate research fellowship that paid my tuition and a stipend of $1,000 a month. I'm sure that Title IX, now being implemented in colleges and universities, opened doors for women like me.

I was entering a male-dominated field. All the PhD students and the faculty in agricultural economics were men, and I shared an office with three men students. There was one woman in the master's program and a few women undergraduates. I felt fortunate to be accepted and encountered no discrimination.

The usual track for a doctorate degree was to complete the course work, pass the preliminary exams, do the research, and write the dissertation. They offered prelims just twice a year, so if you did not pass, this meant your work was delayed. I took the prelims in the spring of 1980, along with six other students. I was the only one to pass!

I thought of Oak Ridge National Laboratory for a job after I got my degree, and natural resource economics was an area of concentration that would fit in with ORNL's research. I initiated contacts with the Economic Analysis Section at ORNL, and they agreed for me to do my research there as part of ORNL's cooperative arrangements with UT.

They assigned me to work with Dr. David Kaserman who held a joint appointment with UT and ORNL. I then asked the UT Department of Agricultural Economics to assign me to Dr. Tom Klint who taught courses in natural resource economics. My graduate committee then became Dr. Klint, Dr. McManus, and Dr. Kaserman.

On a day-to-day basis, ORNL staff operated on an informal, first name basis; therefore, Dr. Kaserman became "Dave." Upon his recommendation, my dissertation research addressed whether energy-conserving investments in a home (such as insulation or a heat pump) would add to the sale price when the home was sold.

School and Work

I researched this question using sales data from the Knoxville Board of Realtors and energy consumption data from the Knoxville Utilities Board in a price equation that included structural and locational attributes. Analysis was done through SAS software on a mainframe computer (before the day of personal computers). I concluded that the housing market does capitalize investments that result in fuel savings. The title of my dissertation was "Housing Market Capitalization of Energy-Saving Durable Good Investments."

ORNL paid the costs for having my dissertation professionally formatted and typed to meet UT's requirements. ORNL also printed my research as an ORNL report. Dave and I submitted several papers to research journals and were pleased to have them accepted.

ORNL paid my expenses to present the research at a meeting of the American Economic Association in San Francisco. It was a great professional experience. I felt I had achieved success—with a PhD and acceptance from colleagues.

The opportunity to see San Francisco was a bonus. I had a beautiful view of the Golden Gate Bridge from my hotel room at the Hyatt Regency.

As a government research facility dating back to the World War II effort, a fence with guards at each gate encloses the ORNL facilities. To enter, you must have a pass. I had the feeling that I was entering a prison. I made the mistake of taking my portable typewriter to work. No one questioned me when I brought it in; when I tried to take it out was another matter. It took some effort to convince the guards that I was not stealing government property.

The 1970s brought about concerns and shortages of energy sources. Therefore, government funding and staffing for research in energy conservation were expanding. One of the problems at ORNL then became one of space. I was in a small office with four desks and barely enough space to get between them. When everyone was in the office, it became too noisy to concentrate.

I enjoyed the camaraderie among staff in the Economics Analysis Section, and I felt accepted as part of the professional staff. My goal was to get a job there when I earned my PhD. It was not to be. During the application and interview process, I was told they preferred staff from prestigious universities like Harvard or Yale over UT. They did offer me a post-doctoral fellowship, but at the same pay level as the research assistantship I had received from UT.

This was the heyday of affirmative action when employers said they wanted to hire more women and minorities, but they couldn't find qualified applicants. Therefore, I expected it would be easy for me to find a job. I applied for job openings at two universities, the University of Florida and the University of Arkansas. The University of Florida interviewed me, but they hired someone else.

Bill was willing to relocate if I got a job elsewhere. However, I realized it was too risky for him to give up his job and benefits at Y-12 for what could be an uncertain situation for me at a university. I then limited my job search to the Knoxville-Oak Ridge area.

Oak Ridge Associated Universities (1980-1982)

I found out about a job in the Training Division at Oak Ridge Associated Universities, where I worked in the 1960s when it was called Oak Ridge Institute of Nuclear Studies. The job was to gather information on nuclear power industry jobs and predict employment needs for the next decade. The Department of Energy and the Institute for Nuclear Power Operations funded this study. ORAU had offered the job to someone who changed plans at the last minute; thus, I got the job on a temporary one-year status.

I began work in December 1980 and would receive my PhD in March 1981. A paper on my dissertation research had already been accepted for presentation at the annual meeting of the American Association for the Advancement of Science in Toronto in January, and ORAU agreed to fund this trip.

Toronto experienced temperatures between 30 and 40 degrees below zero, even colder than usual. Fahrenheit and Celsius temperatures are nearly identical at this extreme cold. Upon reaching the hotel where most meetings took place, I navigated between locations through the underground passageways, resembling a shopping mall experience. The hotel was decorated for Christmas, and from the window in my room I could see ice skaters below. I joined a small group in a van for an excursion to witness the mostly frozen Niagara Falls—a breathtaking sight!

Mr. Earle Cook, a consultant, provided me with valuable background information about the nuclear power industry during my stopover in Washington, DC, on my return from Toronto.

The first step was to collect employment and turnover data from the Institute of Nuclear Power's 60 member utilities, along with projected increases in generating capacity. I analyzed data through econometric models to forecast employment needs by specialized area.

One morning, to meet a deadline, I came to work early. It was still dark and no one else was in the building when I unlocked the door. A short time later, as I was sitting at my desk with my back to the door, someone grabbed me from behind, turning over my chair. The young man told me to do as he said, or he would hurt me. I quickly removed my glasses to keep them from being broken. Holding my arms, he dragged me down the hall and into the restroom. He was ready to force oral sex, but stopped when he heard a door close and someone coming down the hallway. Then he told me to stay where I was to give him time to get away. I waited a short time before leaving the restroom.

Near my office was Marcus, one of my coworkers, who knew something was wrong when he saw the overturned chair. He did not see my attacker as he was leaving the building. I was in a state of shock, and I asked Marcus to call the police. The police had little to go on. They suspected it could have been one of the students in the Training and Technology program who would have had access to the building. Later, they got photographs of these students to see if I could identify one of them as the attacker. I could not, and the police did not arrest anyone.

ORAU staff insisted I go to the hospital emergency room to be checked. Emergency room personnel called my family doctor. He checked my heart rate and blood pressure, which were high as expected, and I had a few bruises. He offered to write me a prescription for medication that would help me calm down, but I didn't think it was necessary. Bill took me home. A friend, Sibyl Nestor, brought me flowers.

In the afternoon, I began to have unexplained vaginal bleeding, so I went to the doctor's office. He assured me that this sometimes happens to a woman following a traumatic event. I went back to work the next day and gradually, I recovered. The *Oak Ridger* reported the story; fortunately, they did not use my name.

Although my employment had been for one year, I worked for 20 months before being given a reduction in force. I then collected unemployment benefits for a few months. My efforts at finding another job were unsuccessful.

Economic System Analysis, Inc. (1983-1985)

Ruth Maddigan, a friend whom I had met at ORNL, and I decided to open a consulting firm specializing in economic topics. We expected to get government subcontracts through our professional contacts in Oak Ridge. Also, Ruth had worked on electricity demand forecasting for rural electric cooperatives, and we saw this as a potential market for our business. We each invested $10,000 as startup funds.

We named the business Economic System Analysis (ESA), had it incorporated, and got our business license. Equipment purchased included an IBM personal computer (they were new at that time, no internet) and furniture for our office. Yes, it was sometimes confusing that we were both named Ruth.

ESA got a small contract with ORNL, and we worked with Science Applications International Cooperation (SAIC) on socioeconomic impacts of closing one of the gaseous plants in Paducah, Kentucky, Portsmouth, Ohio, or Oak Ridge, Tennessee. Old Dominion Electric Cooperative in Richmond, Virginia, gave us a contract for electricity demand forecasting.

Over a short period, it became apparent that Ruth and I had differing opinions and goals about running the business. We agreed it was best for us to go our separate ways. Therefore, Ruth bought out my share of the business for $10,000, which was the amount I had invested.

Science & Technology, Inc. (1986-1988)

I was once again in the job market.

Bill and I had become acquainted with Mr. Bill Joyner through Bill's contacts with others in the civil rights movement. Bill Joyner, a retired military officer, managed the Oak Ridge office for Science & Technology, Inc. (SciTek), a minority-owned consulting firm with headquarters in Huntsville, Alabama. Mr. Joyner suggested I review the government publication that lists requests for proposals (RFP) for government contracts. If I wrote a successful proposal for SciTek and they got a contract, I would have a job.

I wrote a proposal in response to the US Department of Labor's RFP to explore options for a person to use his or her unemployment benefits in starting a small business. We got the contract, which made it possible for SciTek to hire me and an assistant to do the work.

The project soon ran into problems. First, DOL strongly recommended that we hire a specified person with experience in this area as a consultant. SciTek management refused this request. Not surprisingly, after about a year into the contract period, DOL canceled the contract, saying they no longer needed this work.

When DOL canceled our contract, SciTek wanted to transfer me to a project they were doing for the military. I did not want to continue working for SciTek for several reasons. One was that my supervisor wanted to micromanage my work, which made it unnecessarily difficult to get anything done. Another reason was the fact that SciTek management was not giving the Oak Ridge office the support we needed. We didn't have a computer, and it was difficult to get office supplies and other necessary items—we kept running out of toilet paper in the restrooms! I began looking for another job.

Becoming Independent

Pellissippi State Community College (1988-1993, 1996-1999)

Pellissippi State Community College hired me as an adjunct instructor to teach economics courses, one in microeconomics and the second in macroeconomics. Being an adjunct means that you have a contract on a semester-to-semester basis rather than ongoing employment. It also means lower pay. I was fortunate that I was in a position where job satisfaction was more important than money. On the positive side, adjuncts do not have meetings to attend or responsibilities other than teaching.

Economics was required for all students in the business curriculum. In the beginning, the department head, Mrs. Cynthia Dempster, assigned me to evening classes. Most of these students were older and had full-time jobs. Many of them were single women raising children. These were serious students who knew the importance of getting an education. Occasionally, a student would bring her child to class because of a problem with childcare arrangements. I allowed this, although it was against school policy, and I never found it to be a problem. These were school-age kids who would sit quietly with their own books and writing material. I recall a boy, probably about 8 years old, who came to class with his mom. At the end of the class, I asked him how he liked it. He replied with complete candor, "It was boring."

Each student wrote a term paper on a topic related to economics. In the first class I taught, a student wrote her paper on the Chinese economy. My reaction when I read it was that none of my students could have written this! In her references, she listed an article from the journal *Science*. I checked and found that she had lifted entire paragraphs from this source—the most obvious plagiarism I've ever seen!

When Pellissippi changed from a quarter to a semester system, they combined the two courses (micro and macro) into one economics course. This made teaching a little more difficult because we were covering the same material in less time.

I volunteered to work in the Writing Center where students could seek individual help with their papers. Methods of teaching writing had changed radically over the past few years, with less emphasis on grammar, punctuation, and spelling. I gave up this volunteer activity after I realized that all I was doing was editing their papers.

As time went by, the department head assigned me day classes, some on the main campus and some at the Division Street campus. It was good not to have evening classes, but I missed the older, more serious students in evening classes.

I remember having an outstanding male student in a day class who always had a perfect score on any assignment or test. But there were a few students who shouldn't have been in college. Community colleges in Tennessee admit any student who has a diploma from an accredited high school. And some students came to Pellissippi after they had flunked out of UT.

Once a student's parent contacted me. This student, Tracy, had been in my summer class (a shorter, more intense course) and had made a D, and a grade of D would not transfer to UT. I assured this mother that if her daughter enrolled in my fall class, I would give her extra help when she needed it. Tracy returned and brought her grade up to C. During the Christmas holidays, I hired Tracy to help with the open house Bill and I had at our home.

Each semester, a faculty member evaluated adjuncts by visiting a class, and students evaluated them as well. I found the faculty evaluations to be helpful in improving my teaching, and student evaluations could also be helpful. However, the system has its flaws. Students may write whatever they wish and not have to sign their name. That, combined with the administration's goal that 70 percent of students successfully complete courses, created pressures for inflated grades.

Pellissippi initiated a professional development plan for adjuncts; upon completion, a salary increase of 15 percent was given. I worked to complete the plan as soon as possible, and I succeeded! Pellissippi also provided opportunities for training using new technology in the classroom.

At the time I began teaching at Pellissippi, I also taught an economics class for Roane State Community College at their campus in Oneida, about 60 miles north of Oak Ridge. They paid me for travel time and mileage, and I enjoyed the drive during beautiful fall weather. However, I did not want to do this traveling during the winter, and I declined Roane State's offer of another class.

SCHOOL AND WORK

In 1989, the People-to-People organization invited me to join a delegation of US economists to visit the Soviet Union. These delegations bring together professionals who meet with their counterparts in other countries. Our delegation of 25 economists, including three women, spent three weeks in the Soviet republics of Russia, Ukraine, and Moldavia. The trip was enlightening—especially so, as the Soviet Union was on the brink of historic changes.

Figure 19. Red Square with marching soldiers. People stood in long lines waiting to view Lenin's tomb.

During the 1980s, the Soviet economy experienced a decline in gross national product. Soviet economists revealed that their most pressing economic issue was the lack of worker incentive.

They believed the problem stemmed from workers being too far removed from the outcomes of their labor. One person summarized the issue succinctly: "They pretend to pay us, and we pretend to work."

Figure 20. Ruth with one of the hospitable Soviet hosts. They greeted us with flowers, food, and gifts.

Gorbachev, who came into office in 1985, started several economic reforms (perestroika) aimed at correcting the problem of worker incentive. The government decentralized planning to some extent, with more control at the republic and district levels. Gorbachev's most revolutionary change was the introduction of private enterprise into the Soviet system.

School and Work

Practically all Soviet women had jobs outside the home. We observed women doing many jobs, ranging from street cleaning to farm labor. At one of the research institutes, we were told that approximately 40 percent of their scientific and technical personnel were women. Several of the institutes we visited had women department heads, but none served in the top position as director.

Figure 21. Women department heads at a research institute in Moldavia.

This experience enabled me to bring back information and slides to share with my classes. Pellissippi State Community College taped one of my presentations for other classes.

In 1993, near the beginning of the fall semester, Bill suffered a heart attack and other complications. Therefore, I resigned from teaching so that I could care for him at home. Following his death in 1995, it took me some time to decide that I was ready to go back to teaching. I returned to Pellissippi in the fall of 1996.

It was good for me to be back in the classroom after a three-year absence. Fortunately for me, all my assigned classes were now at the main campus on Pellissippi Parkway. It seemed to me that students had changed during the time I was away—they seemed less mature and there were a few discipline problems. They acted like high school students! Then again, the problem might have been that I had aged!

Doug and I were married in 1998. Gradually, I thought about retiring from teaching so that I could pursue other interests, and Doug and I could spend more time in Florida. I resigned at the end of fall semester 1999.

Reflections

I remember asking one of my elementary school teachers how long you could go to school. Her answer was, "As long as you live." I haven't spent my entire life in school, but it has been a large portion of my life, as well as the part of my career that I have enjoyed the most. My niche is in academia.

Sometimes I wonder if I would have been better off to have gone directly from high school to a job and stayed there until I retired. Perhaps my life would have gone more smoothly, and I might have earned about the same amount of money, but it wouldn't have been nearly as interesting! I have come to believe that the benefits of education are much more than earning a living. Education increases your potential for enjoying life.

When I entered the PhD program, I was in a male-dominated field, and I was the first woman to receive a PhD in Agricultural Economics from UT. When I received my degree, there were few women employed in the research firms where I worked. I hope I have made it easier for the women who followed. I'm grateful for the opportunities I've had and those individuals who have helped me along the way.

Grandchildren

Next Generations

I became a grandmother when John and Janice became a couple, and John was a father to Clinton, Janice's son. They were living in Greensboro, North Carolina, when I first met Janice and Clinton. I found Clinton to be a sweet, good-looking boy who was about three years old.

Next came two granddaughters. This must have been God's way of compensating me for not having had a sister or a daughter. I have certainly enjoyed being grandmother to Jessica and Crystal, as well as Clinton.

During a few days' visit around Jessica's birth in 1983, the joy of seeing her as a beautiful small baby was evident, and her parents and brother couldn't contain their pride. There were challenges, as she cried often, and despite our efforts, we couldn't always discern her needs.

Upon my return to the Raleigh airport in the rental car, I had a brief visit with Glenn (Zeke) Paire, my former brother-in-law, to whom I'm grateful for his support of John in his electrician training.

Grandchildren

In 1985 Crystal was born. By that time, John and Janice had bought a house in Rocky Mount, North Carolina, and they were just moving in when Crystal arrived. I drove there and stayed a few days to help them get settled in their new home and to assist with care of the growing family.

Bill was grandfather to David and Laura who lived in Oak Ridge. We enjoyed seeing them grow up and visiting them.

Bill quickly became a good grandfather who was much loved by Clinton, Jessica, and Crystal. He had a special way of dealing with kids. We visited often. The family would come here for Christmas and sometimes the three kids would spend another week, and I would take them back home.

I remember the time that John called to ask if I could get the kids and keep them for a week or so. Janice had a job, and John was recovering from hernia surgery. This turned out to be a pleasant visit for us. We had time to do the things we enjoyed, like swimming and visiting the Children's Museum in Oak Ridge.

When I was driving them home, we went through Morristown, Tennessee, where there is a paper mill. When Jessica noticed the odor coming from the paper mill, she said, "Grandma, Crystal has messed in her pants." I explained that the bad smell was coming from the paper mill. The paper mill remains there today, but they have managed to control the odor.

I took Clinton and Jessica on a trip to Disney World. Crystal seemed too young for the trip. I drove to their house to pick up

Clinton and Jessica. Crystal cried because she wanted to go, too. We drove to the airport in Charlotte and flew to Orlando, Florida.

Then there were the summer visits when the three kids would spend two weeks or more with Bill and me in Oak Ridge. They enjoyed the hot tub, and Bill let them play on the computer. We would go for walks with our dog Blackie down to the lake. I remember giving Jessica a bag of breadcrumbs so that we could feed the geese at the lake. She would now and then take a bite of crumbs for herself and then give some to Blackie. By the time we got to the lake, we didn't have many crumbs left for the geese.

The kids had fun during their visits. They learned how to swim, played in playgrounds, and attended summer camps at the Children's Museum and Camp Fire Girls camp. I remember when I had signed up Jessica and Crystal for a half day at the Children's Museum day camp. When I picked them up the first day, Jessica wanted to know why I hadn't signed them up for a full day. And so, I did.

We also enjoyed many trips to Dollywood and Ogle's Water Park.

During this time, I was teaching at Pellissippi State Community College and I had one or two classes in the summer. Jessica asked why I was teaching in the summer. "You should be spending more time with us," she said. I listened to Jessica and gave up teaching in the summer.

When John and family moved to Maryland, Bill and I would often meet them for a weekend somewhere in Virginia. It was a great way to stay in touch.

Grandchildren

Janice died in a car accident in 1992. I remember when I got the unexpected news of her death. John made plans for a service and burial in North Carolina. I asked my supervisor at Pellissippi State for a week away from teaching so that I could be with John and family. I said that years from now, students wouldn't remember that I hadn't been in class, but my grandchildren would remember that I had been with them.

Following the service and burial for Janice, I went home with John and family and stayed for a week. I was glad to be there to help in some small way. I admire how John and the three children carried on after this tragic event. Clinton, who was now in his teens, soon went to live with his father in North Carolina.

By this time, we had replaced summer visits in Oak Ridge with trips I took with the two girls. First, we went to Disney World. I flew from Knoxville to Orlando; Jessica and Crystal flew from Baltimore to Orlando, and we met at the airport. Other visits included Busch Gardens, Virginia Beach, and Ocean City.

Then there were the trips I gave the girls as a gift for high school graduation. I told Jessica she could choose any place in the US, and she chose Hawaii. I also took Crystal to make up for that first trip to Disney World that she didn't get to go on. When Crystal graduated, she and I chose a week at a dude ranch in Colorado.

I invited the girls to be with me in Nashville for occasions that were special for me. Jessica was there when I received the E Award from the Tennessee Economic Council on Women in 2011. In 2013, Crystal came to Nashville for the book launch of

Tennessee Women of Vision and Courage that I helped compile and edit.

I love and admire my granddaughters as the fine young women they have become. I'm proud of Crystal's service in the military. And I'm proud of my two great-grandsons, Brenner and Maxwell. They, along with my son John and daughter-in-law Elizabeth "Liz," have made my life worthwhile.

Figure 22. John and Liz at wedding of John's daughter, Jessica. (2020)

GRANDCHILDREN

The Greats and Grands

Figure 23. Granddaughter Crystal Blevins served in the US Army, 2003-2008. (2020)

Figure 24. Granddaughter Jessica and Brian Talley at their wedding. (2020)

Figure 25. Four generations; Son John Paire, Granddaughter Crystal Blevins, Great-grandson Maxwell Tilghman, Granddaughter Jessica Talley, Great-grandson Brenner Balog, Great-grandmother Ruth Smiley. (2018)

Figure 26. Great-grandson Brenner John Balog. (2023)

Figure 27. Great-grandson Richard Maxwell Tilghman. (2018)

Figure 28. Eden Talley, daughter of Brian Talley. (2020)

Figure 29. David and Laura Johnson, grandchildren of Robert William Johnson. (1981)

Figure 30. William Arneson, Great-grandson of Robert Willliam Johnson. (2021)

Organizations

Expanding Horizons

Three organizations have influenced my life: the 4-H Club when I was growing up, AAUW (American Association of University Women) during my adult years, and Taoist Tai Chi in the past ten years.

4-H Club (1946-1954)

The symbol of the 4-H Club is a clover, with four leaves representing Head, Heart, Hands, and Health.

The 4-H Pledge
I pledge—
My Head to clearer thinking,
My Heart to greater loyalty,
My Hands to greater service, and
My Health to better living
For my Club, my Community, and my Country

Organizations

The 4-H Club was the only organization or extra-curricular activity, other than sports, available in my elementary school. I joined when I was ten years old. We had monthly meetings during school hours when the county extension agents came. Each member selected projects to work on at home. My projects included food preparation, food preservation, gardening, and home improvement. One year, my Uncle Haskel Hughes gave me a baby pig that I raised as a project, and I sold the pig when it reached its full growth.

Besides the monthly meetings, the 4-H Club sponsored a county-wide Achievement Day held in the Bristol Tennessee High School stadium, a state-wide event called Roundup at the University of Tennessee in Knoxville, and 4-H Congress in Nashville. I attended most of these events, and they certainly expanded my horizons. 4-H motivated me to go to college.

In 1948, when I was 12 years old, I joined a group of 4-H members for a bus trip to Washington, DC, and a week-long stay to see the sights. We stayed in a tourist camp with small cabins and a central bathroom facility. My roommates were two adult leaders and a girl about my age. We visited the usual government buildings and historic sites, and I was impressed at seeing these places for the first time.

One afternoon and evening we went to Glen Echo amusement park where I took my first and only ride on a roller coaster. That ride terrified me. I had enough of that type of thrill to last me a lifetime.

Becoming Independent

The 4-H projects and awards gave me a competitive spirit. I entered and won several county and district awards, and I entered state contests. In 1954, I received a state award to attend Camp Miniwanca, a camp founded by William Danforth of the Purina Corporation, on the shores of Lake Michigan. I flew on a plane from Tri Cities Airport to Michigan. After the two weeks at camp, I flew to Knoxville to attend 4-H Roundup at the University of Tennessee. After a week there, Dad flew in his Cessna plane to Island Airport in Knoxville to bring me back home. And just a few weeks later, I entered UT as a freshman student.

Figure 31. Sullivan County 4-H members at 4-H Roundup, University of Tennessee. Ruth in front row, center. (1953)

Organizations

The year 2023 marked the 100th Anniversary of 4-H Roundup. I contributed to the 4-H Foundation to express my appreciation for what 4-H means to me.

American Association of University Women (AAUW) (1970-present)

In 1970, the AAUW Knoxville Branch awarded AAUW membership to me and three other graduating women seniors at UT. In many ways, AAUW became important to me in the same way as 4-H had been. The mission of AAUW, founded in 1881, is to "advance equity for women and girls through advocacy, education, and research."

After moving to Oak Ridge in 1971, I joined AAUW Oak Ridge Branch. These members became friends and important contacts through the years I have been here. I served as President of the Oak Ridge Branch and State President of AAUW Tennessee. Through my work in AAUW, I received an "E" Award (for Excellence and Equity) from the Tennessee Economic Council on Women in 2011. My granddaughter Jessica was there, making the recognition even more special.

What I'm most proud of is my role in the publication of the book, *Tennessee Women of Vision and Courage,* in 2013. As a project of AAUW of Tennessee, Charlotte Crawford and I raised funds for the book and asked for nominations of women to be included in the book. We selected 22 women for inclusion and recruited 20 Tennessee women authors to conduct the research and write the biographies. We compiled and edited the biographies while marshaling the book to publication. This was a major project, and the book won an Award of Excellence from the East Tennessee Historical Society. Royalties went toward donating a copy of the book to every public high school in Tennessee and scholarships for Tennessee college women to attend the National Conference for College Women Student Leaders (NCCWSL).

I'm grateful to have worked with Charlotte and to have her as a friend. When we launched the book at a meeting of the Tennessee Economic Council on Women in Nashville, granddaughter Crystal's presence added special significance.

Figure 32. Charlotte Crawford and Ruth, co-editors of *Tennessee Women of Vision and Courage*. (2013)

In the process of recruiting writers for the book, I gained many professional contacts throughout the state. I met Patricia

Hope, a local writer, who has become both a colleague and a friend.

I'm grateful to both Charlotte and Patricia for encouraging me to write. It is to their credit that I'm now writing *Becoming Independent*.

Taoist Tai Chi (2014-present)

Tai chi has been an important part of my life for the past ten years. I joined the Oak Ridge group because I thought this form of exercise would be good for my physical health as I go through my eighties. In addition to the physical benefits, I found that tai chi also enhances my mental and emotional health.

I'm part of Taoist Tai Chi, taoist.org, as taught by Master Moy. A tai chi set consists of 108 moves, influenced by martial arts, that a practitioner can complete in about 15 minutes.

I entered a tai chi beginner's class taught by Lalia Wilson, an instructor trained in Taoist Tai Chi. Following completion of the beginner's class, I joined a continuing class that met regularly. Then the pandemic hit and the organization suspended classes.

A short time later, as I was leaving the Oak Ridge Public Library, I ran into Martha Cottingham, one of my tai chi classmates. She invited me to join an informal tai chi group that met in the library parking lot. Group members felt they were minimizing risks of Covid by meeting outdoors and wearing masks. I enjoyed being part of this group that included members I had known in an earlier class and others whom I had just met.

Becoming Independent

The group met three times a week, unless it rained, to practice tai chi. As the weather turned cooler in the fall, we began hoping for an indoor venue.

We were grateful when Albert Good, a tai chi participant and a member of the Jewish Congregation of Oak Ridge, obtained permission for our group to meet in the social room of the synagogue. This is a perfect spot for us to practice tai chi three times a week. And we enjoy a tea break, giving us time to visit and get to know one another.

As we were becoming acquainted, I approached a friendly-looking woman and said, "Hello, my name is Ruth." She returned my hello and said, "My name is Eleanor." I replied, "Good to meet you, Eleanor. Your name will be easy for me to remember because my middle name is Eleanor." She looked both surprised and amused when she said, "And my middle name is Ruth." So, Ruth Eleanor and Eleanor Ruth became friends, due in part to the names we share.

Sometime later, a new guy came to the tai chi class. When we had completed a set and were having a tea break. I said to him, "Hello, my name is Ruth." He said, "Good to meet you. My mother's name was Ruth." Then he told me his name is John. Surprised, I told him, "My son's name is John."

I enjoy knowing tai chi class members and learning about their families, travels, and interests, as well as the names that connect us.

When my husband passed away a couple of years ago, tai chi became a support group for me, along with friends, family, and my church. I appreciate the physical, mental, and emotional benefits I receive from tai chi.

Figure 33. Tai chi group in Oak Ridge.
Back row: Lalia Wilson, Steven Earhart, Louise Ackerman (partially hidden).
Front row: Lyle Bennett, Ruth Smiley, Claudia Earhart, Rebecca Charles, Sandra Barry, Gloria Caton.

My Spiritual Journey

The Power of Faith

The church has always been an important part of my life. When I was growing up, we went to Sunday School at Silver Grove Lutheran Church every Sunday. However, we had church services just once a month. This small congregation was part of a four-church parish, served by one pastor. Members of the church included my grandparents, aunts and uncles, and cousins.

I don't recall that we had Bible study or devotions at home. We accepted religion without question in our family. I was baptized as an infant and confirmed at age 12.

Vacation Bible School (VBS) in the summer was an important part of my upbringing. I attended VBS at Silver Grove, an interdenominational VBS at Weavers Church, and another at the Baptist Church in our community.

Through Sunday School and Vacation Bible School, I learned much about the Bible and church teachings. Several songs stand out in my memory. One is

My Spiritual Journey

Jesus Loves the Little Children

Jesus loves the little children,
All the children of the world.
Red and yellow, black and white, they are precious in his sight.
Jesus loves the little children of the world.

I have thought of this song through the years whenever questions of race and prejudice arise.

As an adult, I have always been a church member, including Methodist and non-denominational, and finally back to Lutheran. Over the years, I've seen churches struggle with topics like divorce, civil rights, women's status, homosexuality, and more. I have seen the churches I have been associated with become more accepting and more liberal, as I have also become.

The concept of God's grace is now central to my belief system. This means that God loves all of us. I find inspiration from the Peace Prayer of St. Francis.

Prayer of St. Francis of Assisi

Lord, make an instrument of Your peace.
Where there is hatred, let me sow love;
where there is injury, pardon;
where there is despair, hope;
where there is doubt, faith;

where there is darkness, light;
and where there is sadness, joy.
O Divine Master,
grant that I may not so much seek
to be consoled as to console;
to be understood as to understand;
to be loved as to love;
for it is in giving that we receive;
it is in pardoning that we are pardoned;
and it is in dying that we are born to eternal life.

In March 2023, I participated in a Via de Cristo spiritual retreat. The purpose of this retreat is to develop Christian leaders.

At the retreat, I received a package of letters from family, friends, and church members. These letters touched and overwhelmed me with emotion and gratitude for these kind words.

I feel this experience strengthened my faith in God, and it helps me in my leadership roles at Grace Lutheran Church, where I am presently a member of the church council. At the church, I organized a flower guild whose members arrange altar flowers for church services. The flower guild has held six annual flower festivals as an outreach to the community. I would like to be remembered for these contributions as a member of Grace Lutheran Church.

Epilogue

My friend Charlotte asked me "What is the theme of your book? Every book should have a theme." It took me just a minute to answer, "Perseverance." I did not begin writing with this theme in mind. It is after recalling my life history that I see perseverance as one of my traits.

Although we had our differences and I went against their wishes in getting married at age 20, I never felt estranged from my parents. I kept in touch. As an example, just a few days after George and I were married, Dad had a birthday. I sent him a small wood-carved rooster as a gift. That rooster was one of the small remembrances I asked for after his death, and that rooster now sits on my desk. I have good memories of the relationship I had with my parents despite differences when I was growing up.

In education, it took three attempts to enter college before I earned a BS degree in 16 years. Education was important to me,

Epilogue

and I continued to graduate school to earn MS and PhD degrees. I have the distinction of being the first woman to receive a PhD from the Department of Resource and Agricultural Economics at the University of Tennessee in 1981.

I experienced some disappointments in my career, but I did not give up. I found my calling in the classroom, and I spent the last years of my employment teaching economics at Pellissippi State Community College.

In my retirement years, I continue my interest in photography, and I am a member of the photography group at Grace Lutheran Church. I have become a writer, an active church member, and a doting grandmother. I enjoy maintaining my home and garden where I have lived for 53 years.

My life is good. I feel that I have persevered to overcome obstacles. I have followed my dreams.

Acknowledgements

I owe a debt of gratitude to friends, Charlotte Crawford and Patricia (Pat) Hope, who inspired me to turn my dream of writing a book into reality. Charlotte and I had previously collaborated on compiling and editing *Tennessee Women of Vision and Courage*, with Pat contributing a piece on Elizabeth Rona, one of the remarkable women featured in the book.

Motivated by the publication of the Tennessee women's book, I began writing about my own life experiences. The encouragement I received from Grace Writers, a group organized by Pat, was instrumental in this journey.

In 2023, I completed the first draft of *Becoming Independent*, and Charlotte undertook the careful and arduous task of editing. As we approached the final stages, we asked Clare Crawford and Kristin Berkey-Abbott to review the manuscript and provide feedback. I am grateful for their insightful suggestions.

Post Rock Press, with Charlotte Crawford as editor, expertly managed the final steps of layout and design to bring this book

Acknowledgements

to publication. I thank Charlotte for her dedication to the myriad details that made the publication of *Becoming Independent* possible.

Publications and Technical Reports

Paire, Ruth Crumley, Master's Thesis: "Home Ownership Attitudes and Housing Satisfactions of Families Who Have Received Assistance Under Section 235 of the Housing and Urban Development Act of 1968," University of Tennessee, June 1971.

Johnson, Ruth C. and B. R. McManus, "A Theoretical Framework for Analyzing Social Costs of the Tobacco Program," *Southern Journal of Agricultural Economics,* pp. 103-106, December 1979.

Johnson, Ruth Crumley, PhD Dissertation: "Housing Market Capitalization of Energy-Saving Durable Good Investments," University of Tennessee, March 1981.

Johnson, Ruth C. and Thomas H. Klindt, "Efficiency of the Housing Market in Capitalizing Returns from Energy-Saving Investments," *Tennessee Farm and Home Science,* pp 31-33, 1981.

Johnson, Ruth C., "Housing Market Capitalization of Energy-Saving Durable Good Investments," ORNL/CON-74, Energy Division, Oak Ridge National Laboratory, July 1981.

Johnson, Ruth C., "Manpower Requirements in the Nuclear Power Industry, 1982-1991," Oak Ridge Associated Universities, September 1982.

PUBLICATIONS AND TECHNICAL REPORTS

Jackson, Jerry R., Ruth C. Johnson, and David L. Kaserman, "The Measurement of Land Prices and the Elasticity of Substitution in Housing Production," pp. 1-12, *Journal of Urban Economics*, 1984.

Johnson, Ruth C., Team Member, "Socioeconomic Assessment: Partial Closure of the Paducah Uranium Enrichment Facility," by Science Applications International Corporation, Oak Ridge, Tennessee, May 1985.

Maddigan, Ruth J., Ruth C. Johnson, and C. A. Maddigan, "The Return on Government Investments," ORNL/PPA/INT-85/3 Report, Oak Ridge National Laboratory, May 1985.

Kaserman, David L., John L. Trimble, and Ruth C. Johnson, "Equilibration in a Negotiated Market: Evidence from Housing," pp. 30-42, *Journal of Urban Economics*, 1989.

Johnson, Ruth C., "A View of the Soviet Union," prepared for Economics classes at Pellissippi State Community College, Knoxville, Tennessee, 1989.

Johnson, Ruth C., "Glenn Crumley Family," *Families and History of Sullivan County, Tennessee, Volume One, 1779-1992*, Holston Territory Genealogical Society, Wadsworth Publishing, 1992.

Crawford, Charlotte and Ruth Johnson Smiley, co-editors of *Tennessee Women of Vision and Courage*, 2013.

Smiley, Ruth Johnson, and Doug Smiley, *Animal Kingdom*, Shutterfly, 2016.

Smiley, Ruth Johnson, "Good Samaritans," p. 124-125, *In God's Hand*, Writers of Grace, 2017.

Smiley, Ruth Johnson, "A Day to Remember," First Place Award in Grace Writers Contest, April 2023.

Smiley, Ruth Johnson, "We Love Oak Ridge," p. 2, *Oak Ridge Neighbors*, May 2023.

Note:

Ruth Crumley Paire, Ruth C. Johnson, and Ruth Johnson Smiley are all the same author.

Media Credits

Cover photo by Ruth Johnson Smiley shows a view of the area surrounding Crumley farm.
Author photo by Reflections and Images Photography (2012)
1. Family Chart, Ruth Johnson Smiley by Charlotte Crawford (2023)
4. Ruth Eleanor Crumley, Osborne Studio (1937)
7. George Paire by Olan Mills (1953)
13. Photo by Ruth Johnson Smiley, selected by Thrivent Financial for their 2013 calendar Photo portrays hymn, "When Morning Gilds the Sky."
29. Charlotte Crawford and Ruth Johnson Smiley by Michael Broyles Photography (2013)

All other photos are in the author's family collection.

1. Family Chart, Ruth Johnson Smiley. (2023)
2. Ruth with parents, Glenn and Grace Crumley, at home of Crumley grandparents. (1939)

Media Credits

3. Historic house in Jonesborough that was once a boarding house. Ruth and parents, Glenn and Grace Crumley, lived here for a brief time in the 1930s. (2022)
4. Ruth Eleanor Crumley. (1937)
5. Ruth Eleanor Crumley. (1939)
6. House on farm in Sullivan County where Ruth grew up. Built by Glenn Crumley in 1940 at a cost of $2,000.
7. Ruth with brothers, Claude and Don Crumley, who now operate the family farm. (2020)
8. George Paire in 1953, the year he entered Bluff City High School. (1953)
9. George Paire with son John at John's 50th birthday party. (2008)
10. Robert William (Bill) Johnson. (1990)
11. Bill and Ruth bought this Oak Ridge house in 1971. Ruth still lives here today. (2024)
12. Doug and Ruth on a hike at Big South Fork National River and Recreation Area. (2013)
13. Photo by Ruth Johnson Smiley, selected by Thrivent Financial for their 2013 calendar. Photo portrays the hymn, "When Morning Gilds the Sky."
14. Arbor in our backyard. (2000)
15. Fishpond in our backyard. (2000)
16. Ebony, the cat adopted by Doug and Ruth. (2021)
17. Ruth and son John Paire. (1959)
18. Ruth (right) with classmates at Bluff City High School commencement. Senator Estes Kefauver spoke. (1953)
19. Red Square with soldiers marching and long lines of people waiting to visit the tomb of Lenin.
20. Ruth with one of the hospitable Soviet hosts. They greeted us with flowers, food, and gifts.

BECOMING INDEPENDENT

21. Women department heads at a research institute in Moldavia.
22. John and Liz at wedding of John's daughter, Jessica. (2020)
23. Granddaughter Crystal Blevins served in the US Army, 2003-2008. (2020)
24. Granddaughter Jessica and Brian Talley at their wedding. (2020)
25. Four generations: Son John Paire, Granddaughter Crystal Blevins, Great-grandson Maxwell Tilghman, Granddaughter Jessica Talley, Great-grandson Brenner Balog, Great-grandmother Ruth Smiley. (2018)
26. Great-grandson Brenner John Balog. (2023)
27. Great-grandson Richard Maxwell Tilghman. (2018)
28. Eden Talley, daughter of Brian Talley. (2020)
29. David and Laura Johnson, grandchildren of Robert William Johnson. (1981)
30. William Arneson, Great-grandson of Robert William Johnson. (2021)
31. Sullivan County 4-H members at 4-H Roundup, University of Tennessee. Ruth is front row, center. (1953)
32. Charlotte Crawford and Ruth, co-editors of *Tennessee Women of Vision and Courage*. (2013)
33. Tai chi group in Oak Ridge. Back row: Lalia Wilson, Steven Earhart, Louise Ackerman (partially hidden). Front row: Lyle Bennett, Ruth Smiley, Claudia Earhart, Rebecca Charles, Sandra Barry, Gloria Caton.

About the Author

Ruth Johnson Smiley, a descendant of 1780s German settlers, grew up on an East Tennessee farm. She holds degrees from the University of Tennessee, Knoxville, where she became the first woman to earn a PhD in Agricultural and Resource Economics. With experience at Oak Ridge National Laboratory and teaching economics at Pellissippi State Community College, her career bridges academia and research. She received the Tennessee Economic Council on Women's Award for Excellence and Equity in 2011 for her advocacy for women and girls. Smiley co-edited *Tennessee Women of Vision and Courage*, an anthology of historic Tennessee women.

www.ingramcontent.com/pod-product-compliance
Lightning Source LLC
Chambersburg PA
CBHW070541090426
42735CB00013B/3038